Maritime History

Sacred to their Memory

by John Jefferies

A Very Special Maritime History Book
Compiled by J.A. Jefferies
Published by J.A. Jefferies & R. Levy

Printed by Juniper House of Print, Lawford, England.

FOREWORD

This is a book that every yachtsman and in fact everyone will want to have on their bookshelves when their yachts are stored away for the winter.

Every page holds it's memories, most certainly for myself, being fortunate to have lived through this era of classical schooners, great rigged yachts and of course the J. class.

Being able to photograph all these fine yachts, and meeting their owners and crews over a period of sixty years, I recall a skipper saying to his owner on board "Would you like to take the helm sir" - the owners reply - " I never take anything before lunch".

This book by John Jefferies will be a classic.

Keith Beken F.R.P.S.

Keith Beken F.R.P.S.

(Sadly died February 2007 whilst this book was being prepared for print)

J.J. (centre) with Kenneth Beken (right) and Beken Co. Director Peter Mumford outside famous marine and maritime photographers Beken of Cowes I.O.W.

1st of October 2006

It is a sad fact that all too often a person's knowledge is lost to the world when they depart this life. My new friend "JJ", John Jefferies, is determined that this will not happen to the remarkable information that he can recall about the men who sailed and served on the great racing yachts of his era. This strong desire is held partly for the respect he feels for those he knew in those times, and partly for the benefit of current and future generations of yacht racing enthusiasts. So "JJ" set about the monumental task of committing his remarkable knowledge paper, print and publication. Against the odds of an unfortunate stroke and, not to put it in an unkindly light, an unusual literary style he has already written and published one book crammed with fascinating facts and recollections of life on board the big yachts of yesteryear. I was both surprised and honoured when he telephoned me to ask if I would write this preface for a second edition of his work, which appears with even more facts, stories and pictures. I admire "JJ" for his dogged determination shown in this venture, ably and generously assisted by his friend Ron Levy. Thank you both for keeping an important part of yachting history for all of us.

Bruce Moss, Hon. Librarian and Archivist, RHYC.

J.J. presenting a copy of this book to Commodore Terry Corner at The Royal Harwich Yacht Club.

His Worshipful The Mayor of Colchester Cllr. Terry Sutton endorses J.J.'s memorial maritime book.

It was an honour to meet J.J, and a privilege to see some of his lifetime's collection of photographs, letters and other items, which embrace many aspects of maritime history. J.J. has spent several years putting these priceless treasures together in his impressive book, and has entwined them with true-life stories of tragedy, adventure, foreign lands and new friends - being all part of life at sea. I am proud to endorse J.J.'s tribute to all the seafarers and others who have touched his life.

Cllr. Terry Sutton - Mayor of Colchester 2005.

I have known J.J. for about six years. But it was only recently that I became aware of the extent of his dedication to completing his maritime history book. As a fellow writer, I became drawn into his fascinating world, assisting him by proof reading and preparing his text for the printers. This is a truly exceptional book, written in a unique style. John writes as he speaks, and the book is richer for that. I have enjoyed our meetings and viewing some of J.J.'s collection, which would make many history books on Maritime and Military 1st World War.

Ron Levy - Colchester Borough Councillor.

Tribute to J.J. (Maritime Historian)

The author of this book John Jefferies, affectionately known as 'J.J.' is my maternal cousin.

As children, we would spend many happy hours visiting our grandmother and the fifty plus cousins who lived alongside the River Itchen, which had been the childhood home of our respective mother, and of course, home to many of the crew of the Titanic.

As daughters of the late Harold Stroud, first mate of the royal racing cutter Britannia, 1931-36, my sister Eileen Meegan and I, give love and thanks to JJ for his lifetime work to ensure that the memory of all the mariners, whatever their rank, will never die.

Elizabeth Taylor E.N., R.G.N., R.S.C.N.

I first met JJ some eight or nine years ago during Cowes week, when he came to the Regatta Office where I worked on the information staff.

Since then I have to respect both his encyclopedic knowledge and the deep love of those yacht sailors of an earlier age. It gives me great pleasure to wish my wife's cousin success for this book and thanks for sharing his life's work with us.

Michael Taylor
Eastleigh, Southampton
May 1999.

OUR SAILORMAN KING

King George was more than a respected Monarch, he was a trusted and beloved friend, the real father of his far flung subjects, or as he himself once phrased it, "the head of this great and wide spread family...". He was a man who never spared himself, and whose personality, devotion to duty, plain sincerity, modesty, human kindliness and understanding firmly established the Throne on the surest of all foundations - the hearts of the people.

It was King George's desire, too that Merchant vessels and fishing craft were included in the Spithead Jubilee review - his special wish that representative Masters and Skippers attended on board the Royal Yacht for presentation by the Prince of Wales. It was no idle gesture; but a genuine desire to do honour to Sea Services, to which the country owed so much.
He was brought up as a sailor, and a sailor he remained until the end of his life. Nothing pleased him more than to be at sea with the Fleet, or sailing at Cowes in the Britannia. He knew everything that went on in the Navy, and the liveliest concern for its welfare. Many of the flag officers, particularly those who had been his term-mates in the training ship Britannia, were his personal friends. He never forgot an old shipmate.

The King, on his regular visits to Cowes, found deep pleasure and enjoyment in sailing. Beside being Admiral of the Royal Yacht Squadron, he was patron of many Royal Yacht Clubs.

God rest King George.

God bless his memory, including all our forsaken masters and our mariners of England:

God saw when the footsteps falter,

When the pathway had grown too steep

So he touched the drooping eyelids,

And he gave His loved one sleep.

He is resting so sweetly in Jesus now,

And the wide sea will sail no more,

His soul is now anchored in the haven of rest

And with Jesus he is safe in the haven for evermore.

HM King George V was called to higher circles in January 1936.

Captain Tom Diaper

Our family visited Captain Diaper and his lady wife pre-World War II. Mrs Diaper became totally blind and died and was laid to rest in Peartree Cemetery on the 1st day of World War II. Sadly we were unable to attend Mrs Diaper's funeral service. Our friends next door to Captain Tom was skipper Ben Parker, brother of my uncle Horace Parker. Ben lost his treasured wife and three young children in the first air raid upon Southampton City Docks; one daughter, who is known to J.J. was saved through running on an errand for her mother.

Harkaway leading the West Solent Class

HARDY SONS OF THE SEA

Is this group of five brothers a record?

Reading from left to right they were Messers. William, Joseph, John, Arthur and Stephen Barbrook. The eldest was 83 years of age, and the youngest 69, and their ages total 381 years.

All were hale and hearty. At the early age of nine they started dredging with their father, the late Mr. Joseph Barbrook who lived to the age of 86, and have followed the sea either dredging or yachting. They were born in Tollesbury Essex and all resided there. Capt Stephen Barbrook had been captain of Mr. W. Leuchars' racing yachts for 20 years and the last 10 years of his steam yacht. During that period he was 'lent' to King Alfonso of Spain and Sir James Pender to captain their yachts. All five brothers displayed great independence of character and were very much respected in Tollesbury and further afield. With mostly local sailormen serving on board that famous racing yacht Bryn Ill which was broken up on the hard in Brightlingsea in 1908.

Stephen Arthur Barbrook	*January*	*1932*	*Age 69.*
Arthur	*May*	*1935*	*Age 74.*
John	*March*	*1941*	*Age 85.*
Joseph	*January*	*1943*	*Age 91.*
William Joseph	*November*	*1932*	*Age 83.*

All interred in Tollesbury Cemetery.

The late Captain Stephen Barbrook of Tollesbury was indeed a crack-racing master and whilst serving on board 15-metre class racing yacht Hispania owned by H.M. Alfonso, King of Spain. During the racing season in 1907 Sailorman Supreme, the late Joseph Ruffell Snr. of Brightlingsea was one of her serving crewmembers. He had also served on board the world famous Shamrocks in 1901 and 1902 and in 1907 a very young lad, a nephew of King Alfonso had fallen overboard and would have drowned had it not been for the fact that Sailorman Joseph Ruffell was a most powerful swimmer and diver. The lad was caught up under the rudder bar somehow with a strong running tide. Through saving the lads life he was made a hero overnight for which he was awarded a solid gold medal from H.M. King Alfonso of Spain. Joseph Ruffell carried a long scar upon his face for the rest of his life through his act of love for a fellow human being. As a lad I would often visit the warm home of Mr. and Mrs. Ruffell with my late neighbour from childhood days, Mr. George Ruffell, of late, whose father, Mr. Fred Ruffell was in battle with my father serving in the rifle brigade during the 1st World War. The late Mr. Ruffell was also, prior to the 1st World War, a leading fireman on board Sir Thomas Lipton's SY Erin mastered by the late captain Dick Pascoe of Cowes, Isle of Wight. Mr. Billy Ruffell, of local, a retired marine engineer who served RN 2nd World War also being one of the grandsons of Joseph Ruffell. We often wonder what became of all the old photographs and Spanish newspaper reports that filled the room at Mr. Ruffell's John Street cottage that no longer exists but was situated next to my Brightlingsea Grandparents.

During the 1908 yachting season sailorman Joseph Ruffell joined the 1000 ton SY Varuna owned by gentleman Mr. Eugene Higgins of New York with a crew of 70 officers and ratings under the command of Captain Traylor of Wivenhoe, 1st mate Mr. Kidby of Wivenhoe, 2nd mate, with 13 years service Mr. Victor Underwood, local. Sadly this fine luxury yacht foundered upon the rocks in dense fog down off the Madeira coast. She was a total loss close upon her 13th birthday. Sailorman Joseph Ruffell sadly lost his gold medal, sailorman Billy Bird of Wivenhoe lost his life trying to swim for the shore. I must add, with the greatest respects that Captain Traylor who resided next door to the Greyhound at Wivenhoe had picked up a pilot to assist through this hazardous spot and after returning safely home with

S.Y. Varuna

The Crew of Steam Yacht 'Varuna'. Mainly Wivenhoe Men - Aboard The Yacht.
S.Y. 'Varuna' - Twin screw and with schooner rig was built by A & J Inglis at Glasgow in 1896 for Mr Eugene Higgins.
Dimensions L.O.A. 300ft. Beam 35.3ft. Draft 17.3ft. Although the vessel was owned by an American and registered in New York, she spent most of her time in European waters until she was wrecked in Madira in 1909.
Captain Mr Traylor - Wivenhoe. 1st Mate Mr Kidby - Wivenhoe, 13 years service on the day.
2nd mate Mr Victor Underwood with13 years service on the day.

S.Y. Varuna on rocks at Madeira

most local crew members plus four good fisherman/yachtsman from Emsworth, a very quaint place, he wrote to his yacht owner and asked for a reference. In return a photograph of SY Varuna was sent to Captain Traylor, from America, of the vessel sitting on top of the rocks as a total loss. Regretfully, with heartfelt sympathy as a maritime author it is a sad story founded upon facts but this photograph gave Captain Traylor a massive heart attack and he died the following day. So let us pray my lifetimes maritime works and recording of our heritage is most vital and most sacred to all masters and mariners not only for their sakes but also of their families. The smack Greyhound was built at the back of the Greyhound Public House in Wivenhoe in 1884, built and owned by members of the local Barber family. My friend Richard Harman, known as Dick, who served RN during the 2nd World War also dedicated many years serving on board the Clacton on Sea lifeboat and he was also a serving coxswain retired. Dick is well known and respected amongst the barge and smack owners association. He was well known for racing his own lovely sailing smack ADC over the many years of our friendship and happy times on board Nemo II, which Dick owned for several years. Dick and his late brother Bob always held a love/hate relationship towards old smacks when in the good old days the hard earned livelihood of fishing, like many of my own forebears were half starved to death and the other half were drowned. Charles Barber of Brightlingsea was master/owner of Greyhound and on 3rd September 1884 with his two young sons, Theodore aged 16 and Walter aged 14 they all perished when a 2000-ton steamship ran down the smack in thick fog out through the Swin. Their bodies were recovered and I myself often say a private prayer at their graveside in All Saints Cemetery. Dick often talks to me of how his own late father remembered the tragic news of the Greyhound being brought to the door and in the trauma how his grandmother dropped a large kettle of boiling water over his father's brother Charlie, aged 2 years (named after Charles Barber) and scolded him so badly that the flesh left his ribs. This brother died aged 21 in hospital at Mile End, London. Dick's grandfather, William Benjamin Harman went from London with a sack barrow and pushed the body all the way back to Colchester where a Clacton carrier, with horse and cart, gave them a free ride home to Clacton for a Christian burial, this was during the good old days.

Tollesbury.

Having known many of the grand mariners from this quaint and friendly Essex village from man and boy.

Knowing the good fishermen come yachtsmen when many who fetched their harvest from the sea pre 2nd World War and post war into Brightlingsea, knowing and respecting many whom late in life became watch keepers on board the 32 laid up ships upon the river Blackwater in 1957, my own maritime father included. Myself with a fellow mariner, Mr. Gordon Scott retired coasting mariner. We had a most respected gentleman to thank for our positions of employment, late Mr. Johnny Fieldgate RN 2nd World War. Shipping broker of Field Gates Dock Brightlingsea and Colchester. A true gentleman with much love and respect towards my lifetimes recordings. We lived on board one of the Shell Tankers, SS Helicina. Captain Partridge was her master, a most likable and kind gentleman, with a crew of 48 men, British officers and Chinese, likable and kind, most friendly crewmembers, we all got on well together. Gordon and I worked an ex-Trinity House pilot cutter which was owned by local firm, James & Stone and we tendered for the officers and Shell personnel to and from the Mersea shore and running into Brightlingsea. Steam Yacht Media was Mastered by Heroic Master mariner Captain Charles Pitt, who served on board the Shamrock as a young sailorman. Being the Grandfather of a respected Gentleman known to J.J., Mr John Pitt, whose late son Tim is also a qualified master Mariner.

After the 2nd World War had gladly ended, it was just on the toss of a coin by late skipper Percy Howe of Tollesbury, home Lymington, the favourite place of he and his wife Agnes, to see if my friend, skipper Malcolm McGregor RNR retired mariner, or I, should have the deck boys position on board the fabulous yawl rigged yacht Wayward III. An extremely kind gentleman, Mr. Jameison CBE, a company director of Shell Oil Co, owned this yacht. Skipper Percy Howe in 1934 and 1937 had been a serving sailorman on board Endeavour and Endeavour II under the command of the famous captain George Williams. 1st mate Wally Day RI, 2nd mate Bill Taw RI, all of Southampton. Endeavour II 1937, 2 serving sailormen the late Stan Bishop and Reg Tillett of Brightlingsea. But that is another story waiting to be told with every old photograph plus all household names nationwide.

June 1935 a gloom was cast over the whole village of Tollesbury when the sad news reached that maritime village of the sudden death of Captain Isaac Rice of East Street. He died on board the yacht Seabird, lying at Southampton owned by gentleman Sir John Humphreys. Captain Rice was only aged 46 and had mastered the beautiful steam yacht SY Anglia, also owned by Sir John having been his yachtmaster for many years. During the 1st World War he served on board the Troopship SS Berina. Captain Rice being a merchant seaman passed his master mariner qualification during the 1st World War. In the year 1922 he was master of the schooner yacht Dwyn Wyn owned by the late Mr. R. Rellilons and sailed out to Hong Kong. The yacht became becalmed in the Red Sea for three whole weeks and ran very short of provisions. Captain Rice's own maritime, member of family nine years later - he was a lifetime mariner and also a qualified yacht master, decided to join the steam yacht Media as 1st mate, this was to be his final cruise prior to retirement from the sea. He sadly lost his life during a mistral in the Gulf of Lyons in 1926. I must add that a most heroic sailorman of Tollesbury who, as far as I know has never been mentioned for the vital role he took whilst lashed to the wheel on board SY Media, the late Mr. Charles Wash Snr. Through his skills of A1 sailormanship he helped to save the yacht, the owner and all his guests on board during their ordeal in the Gulf of Lyons, not a very nice place to be at the best of times. As the author I am talking from my own maritime experiences. SY Media was classed as a bad omen and she was laid up in Camper & Nicholson's yacht yard in Northam, Southampton for 11 years. Northam, being my mothers native home and at one time having 19 brothers and sisters. All of my uncles, of late were seafarers MN and RN and my mother had also worked at sea on board liners with my late, loveable Auntie Nora. Their favourite ship was the Liner SS France.

Mr. George Durrant of late spent much time at sea as a younger man but with a famous foreman rigger of Camper & Nicholsons named Mr. Wally Long, retired. A man who had worked on all the famous yachts and America's Cup challengers. Mr. Durrant, a much respected man whom I had known since my childhood days, and from my own yachting career. I myself spent much time, during fitting out and laying up periods at Mr Durrant's home with his lady wife. Mr. Durrant had served Camper & Nicholson's fine yard for 38 years, 32 as standing foreman rigger. Mr. Durrant moored all the famous yachts with his pleasant gang of riggers, men being also seafarers whom were all known and respected by JJ. Mr. Durrant was in charge when SY Media was moored up in 1926. Most yachts of large size were towed by one of the Southampton city steam tugs.

On board MY Virginia RYS 1949-1954 the late Mr. Fred Rice of Tollesbury served as mate for one season for a Mediterranean cruise. ST Canute mostly always towed us. Gentleman Mr. Harry Spencer of Spencer Engineering and Rigging, Cowes, Isle of Wight. Friend Ken and I much enjoyed our jovial hour spent together for a nautical yarn during our Cowes, Isle of Wight visits. Sorry Mr. Harry, I was not well enough to come and visit you, Sir, when you came to West Mersea and prepared Sailing Yacht Hispania and towed her away to be rebuilt. I am led to believe by my seafaring friend, Mr. Alan Mole, whose home and family was indeed Hispania for many years lying on the houseboat flats (ancient rights) at West Mersea, Essex. The late Don Mole, a friend whom I would like remembered, of West Mersea, a man of the sea. His life was spent fishing and barging, being a brilliant navigator. Don is gone but will never be forgotten by his family members and his many seafaring friends, his good shipmate, Mr. Ron Eagling included. Manager Mr. Peter Martin, of Spencer rigging, as a lad was under the wing of Mr. Durrant in Camper & Nicholson's yacht yard. Spencer rigging loft is just outside this fabulous yacht yard, which is now known as Shamrock Quay. Just down Lower William Street in Northam where at one time I had 58 cousins on my mothers side of her Northam family and my late respected uncle, Harold Stroud of Whitstable, Kent was indeed the 1st mate on board the Royal Racing Cutter Britannia from 1931 unit 1936. Mr. Peter Martin and his team of riggers were very much involved with the rigging on board the fabulous J Class Velsheda that is restored to perfection and glory. A work of art by the human hand and it was an honour for me to be invited on board on her completion. My invite by her proud sailing master Captain Simon Bolt. Thank you sir, JJ.

Rigger George Durrant, most of his rigging skills were taught to him by an Al rigger by the name of Danny Houston, a Wivenhoe mariner by birth I believe. A man who in 1911 cut away, down in Camper & Nicholson's fine yacht yard in Gosport one of the masts on board the 3 master 350 ton schooner Margarita, the mast was damaged and when the mast was positioned and cut it fell clean overboard and would not have broke or cracked an egg upon the rail on Margarita. Witnessed by two serving members on Britannia, the late Fred and Johnny Turner of Wivenhoe.

Come winter of 1926 Mr. Durrant was working aloft on board the Phantome owned by the gentry folk, Guinness family. Mr. Durrant was shattered as Danny Houston became ill and was frozen in snow aloft with cold. He went home and sadly died. A point of maritime interest, the fabulous yacht Margarita 380 ton was built in 1911 at Camper & Nicholson, Gosport. Her solid lead keel weighed 100 tons and was run in one smelt. Her Master was a captain Billy De'ath of Brightlingsea. 1st mate Big Sid Martin, a close neighbour who carried a double hernia for life from clearing Margarita's anchor and cable when entangled with a Man of War anchor cables. Many old photographs are held within the JJ collection.

Tollesbury masters and mariners, respected hardy men of the sea. Some names of sailormen: Hubert Heard perished at sea on board Jarvis Bay. Frank Peticon, Hector Ingate, Mr. Seabrook lost their young lives amongst fellow officers and serving seamen on board the SS Rawlpindia. My friend, the late Mr. Cyril Coates being a 1937 Endeavour crewmember lost a brother at sea RN, Lieutenant. Cyril was called to rest 17th July 1998 aged 86 years. His late, charming wife Ruby showed warmth and kindness on my many visits during the bad winter of 1957, I myself along with fellow mariner, Mr. Gordon Scott who also lost two brothers in war. Ken Scott was killed at Anzio and Alf Scott was lost at sea aged 26 years when the master and all hands perished without trace on board one James of Southampton deep sea tugs sailing out of Southampton October 22nd, 1940 at 11.00 pm on a Sunday night. The Captain's son missed certain death through taking his young lady to the Odeon Cinema in Southampton and arriving just two minutes late to board ST Sea Gem and seeing her sail. His father was strict for time. During this young mans Army days he was based in Brightlingsea for a short time. I would like to add barge skipper, late Reg Scott, a lifetime barge skipper, starting in sail who also helped to rescue young troops off the beaches of Dunkirk. I had sailed myself with skipper Reg between my yachting career also with good coasting masters of late, Fred Scales, Joe Gould and Gerald Edward Ashcroft, my friend and shipmate born 27th February 1922, he died 26th September 1990. The inscription on his tombstone in All Saints Churchyard, Brightlingsea. Home is the sailor, home from the sea. Coasting master David Heinkel, gentleman of late Mr. John Hobins, Maldon, director of shipping I had served on board his vessels. He loved his sailing barge, The Lord Roberts, and coasting vessel MV Peterna was lost. He owned MV Wallbrook and MV Beverlybrook. As a young man skipper Gerry Ashcroft was a naval rating and became a sub lieutenant. On June 6th 1944 had sailed across to the Normandy beaches to save 150 lives. He sailed with gentleman Mr. Lightoller who was 2nd officer on board RMS Titanic. This gentleman's yacht was named MY Sundowner. She has been well cared for by the Chatham Dockyard Trust and restored. Mr. Lightoller was well known and greatly respected by my own maritime father and mother. In April 1912 140 of her close Northam schoolfriends had lost a relative overnight, a father in most cases. Mr. Lightoller also mastered yachts with far too many stories of the sea to be told. However, during my lifetime there were indeed happy and sad times. During my days working to and from the many ships laid on the river Blackwater in 1957, 32 in all some tanker masters I can recall who were extremely kind to Gordon and I were captains Clayton, Partridge, Shaw, Bonnywell, Bambry. We got on very well with all the many Tollesbury mariners who many were watch keepers serving week and week about on board the ships. There was my friend Ted Heard jnr who served Shamrock V as ships carpenter in 1930. He also served the big racing yacht Astra as carpenter, and Endeavour in 1937. Ted was called to rest on the 17th February 1999 aged 93 years. Also serving was sailorman Victor Potter Snr. of Tollesbury DSM, fisherman - yachtsman who was mate on board Lord G. Soames, a colonel in the Blues and Greys Regiment, private yacht Dawn Star. Victor Potter was a serving crewmember as a young seaman,

Late Captain Hedgeley of the Hythe, Southampton was master of the yacht Dawn Star and my shore going pals from my happy yachting days, Ned Stevens, Fred Honey and strong man Andrew Steer, all of Port Isaac, Cornwall, were indeed also serving crewmembers. The Admiralty picked up Ned and Fred being RNVR on the first day of war. I myself sailed with jovial shipmates of Port Isaac, to mention a few Fred and Frankie Grills, Little Morley, Jack Spry, Gaggy Bill Hoskins, Jimmy Peters, Henry Lugg, Dan Mutton Shamrock V boatswain 1930, Endeavour boatswain 1937.

Navie Musset served as watchkeeper on board the ships in 1957 and was indeed one of everyones favourite characters, easy to get on with. His son, Keith, skippered a sailing yacht during the 1960's and we often linked up whilst cruising down the glorious West Country. Navie was a superb fisherman/yachtsman the same as my friend the late Cyril Heard who was serving on board the fabulous 600 ton schooner Creole, approx. 1953. His brother, gentleman, the late Mr. Fred Heard served as 1st mate and Navie and Cyril also served on board the laid up ships in 1957. Navie was called to rest in his 90th year and he loved trawling until the very end. During his life upon God's earth Navie was still as strong as an ox, his favourite saying 'one is not pulling on the rope until ones feet are pulled through the deck.' A story Navie once told me was when as a P.O.W. working in the salt mines during the 1st World War a guard was very cruel to Navie and his friend, they waited their time and Navie knocked him clean cold. His chum nodded and opened a large sized furnace door and between them they picked the guard up and hove him into the furnace and cremated him alive. He was not missed.

As stated within my recordings many and much have come into my life, both happiness and sadness being involved. As a serving seaman with Trinity House when the three ships, SS Caribbean, SS Brandinburgh and SS Nicky all came to grief down off the Varne Shoal June 1970. The loss of life at sea is so cruel; it often provides a good harvest of fish but then reaps its reward of men in return. In 1962 I was serving mate on board the, late gentleman Mr. McKay's MY Giroflee, Southampton based. The late captain, Thomas Watts, a much respected man was master, a Padstow mariner, home Southampton. He was indeed the sailorman crewmember on board Endeavour in 1934 America's Cup Challenge who wrote the protest letter on behalf of the crewmembers for a bonus of £50.00 per sailorman, danger money, to cross the Atlantic when 13 crewmembers resigned over the dispute to sail. Yes it is often recorded 14 but one man did return overnight and was nicknamed Tom Dooley, like the old song Captain Watts would sing to me, only in fun. Our good friend, engineer Dick Farrow from St. Ives, Cornwall being a nephew of the only survivor from the St. Ives lifeboat tragedy. To my own way of thinking Sir Thomas Sopwith had every right to stick to his principles owing to the facts. All the crew, under the command of Captain G. Williams, 1st mate W. Day 1934 had one and all, agreed to sail prior to this dispute by signing a Board of Trade Agreement. JJ knows all these family crewmembers. Sailorman Phil Williams, a brother of Captain George Williams was a serving sailorman and sadly died summer 1985 soon after my last visit. He was aged 78 years. Captain Williams sadly died on board Endeavour II in September 1937 during the typhoon on the homeward voyage and he was buried at sea 150 miles west of the Azores and it was Phil who had to announce to the crew that the sailing masters life was over; he had seen the harbour lights and regretfully raced us home. Sir Thomas Sopwith with his brand new motor yacht Phillante, which was commanded by the late Captain Donald McKillopp, from the Outer Hebrides. He was known and highly respected by JJ. MY Philante, carried 80 private crewmembers and when in October 1937 Endeavour and Endeavour crewmembers sailed into Gosport to receive a heroes return Sir Thomas showed and gave overwhelming kindness to all the families involved, allowing his private luxury yacht to be used on this joyous occasion as a floating hotel. Late Jack Frost of Tollesbury was Chief Steward and his late brother Frank was 2nd steward.

Sir Thomas Sopwith, aviator, pioneer, inventor, designer, who was called to higher circles January 27th 1989 aged 101 years. I myself, as a lad, saw the building of this magnificent yacht, built and launched by Camper & Nicholsons Northam Yard, Southampton. She was so large that her bow overhung the pavement right hand side down in Lower William Street. Special permission was obtained from city officials of the fabulous city of Southampton. Many of my 58 cousins and I, in 1937, would go down to Camper & Nicholson's with our lovely old Granddad Alf Harfield's wheelbarrow to pick up off cuts of timber for our grandfather's fire down at No. 8, Lower York Street, Northam this being how at one time, all the lovely old houses once stood. We also collected timber for all our relatives in what was known as 'Happy Northam'.

Within my recordings I do mention the sad and happy times through life, so back for a moment to 1962. I was the mate on board MY Giroflee on the Saturday 27th July 1962 to be precise. My wife, Jean was caring for two small, happy lads for the mother who had been in hospital for two weeks. My wife had purchased, for Tony and Terrence Squires, aged 7 and 3 years, new T-shirts, shorts and plimsolls from the late Mr. Southerwood's newsagents and sweet shop etc. This was a shop full of beach wear and toys, a lovely shop run many years by Mr. and Mrs. Southerwood and it was situated on the corner of Sydney Street, (which is now the Nationwide Building Society). My wife had returned Tony and Terrence to their mother, Peggy, at midday, and most sadly they wandered off down Morse's Lane, local in the afternoon down Morse's Lane, now near the Five ways Co-op and entered to play and paddle in the disused sand pits, twenty feet deep, near Mr. Farley's farm. They both sadly drowned. The late police sergeant, Mr. Ken Frances, a gentleman whom I greatly respected and admired, being a very strong swimmer and diver recovered their bodies with the help of PC (retired) Mr. Robert Cook. A man who has always exchanged kind words with myself, Mr. Farley, also cared for these two young children by wiping them dry with towels and covering them up with blankets. This I was told when arriving home. Sadly when Sergeant Ken Frances was posted to Clacton, still a kind and caring man to fellowmen, he helped to start a gentleman's car by pushing it to start. Being the powerful man that he was it regretfully gave this kind and caring man a massive heart attack from which he sadly died. God bless his memory.

The good mariners of Tollesbury many served on board the world famous Shamrocks. Theodore Lewis, man of sail was the serving 2nd mate on board the 23 metre Shamrock under the command of the late famous captain Isaac Sycamore who died 19th April 1930 aged 74. Late sailorman Tom Sampson was 87 years old in 1965. His Tollesbury shipmates on board the famous Shamrock II were, sailorman Ned Heard and Will Riley A1 sailormen. Tom was world travelled at sea and in 1903 there was indeed a tragedy on board Shamrock when the yacht was racing at Hunters Quay, on the Clyde. A squall blew up and snapped her 160 ft. mast. Sadly Mr. Collier, a steward from Wivenhoe was crushed and drowned, not to be seen again. A most sad day

Fabulous 1920's life shot of the 23 metre Shamrock taking the lead racing on the Clyde. On the left is Colonel Neile, Sir Thomas Lipton's advisor. Then 1st mate Captain Ned Heard of Tollesbury, famed for being the master of Shamrock V in 1930 and master of Mr Paul's Astra. It was a sad day for all on board, family and all our neighbourly friends when sailorman George Henry Lewes drowned from Astra whilst racing out of Southend, aged 51 years, on 6th June 1935. Famous Captain I. Sycamore at the helm. Also a most brilliant Tollesbury man of sail, sitting down on the right, serving 2nd mate Theodore Lewis.

for master and crew and all concerned as the famous sailing master, late captain Robert Wringe who died aged 67 years at his Brightlingsea, Sandy Hook, home February 14th 1924, being my maritime father's uncle. He was married to my grandfather's sister Emily. Edward, the brilliant 1st mate was an A1 sailorman with nerves of steel. The late captain Ned Heard serving 1st mate, at the time of the tragedy when sailorman supreme Theodore Lewis was washed overboard and sadly drowned off Seaview, Isle of Wight 2nd April 1924. Gone but not forgotten in the JJ Collection.

The late Jack Wash RNVR 2nd World War was serving on board the fabulous luxury yacht MY Narcissus' under the Admiralty. Jack, being a shipmate on board with two of the Stroud brothers of Whitstable in Kent being also brothers of my late Uncle Harold Stroud RNVR. The yacht, on Admiralty service, was named HMS Gieve where on board many of her gallant crewmembers were sadly killed and several were also wounded on May 29th 1940. Dunkirk became a trap for British Forces and Europe and MY Narcissus was renamed HMS Gieve by the Admiralty, believed to be in honour of the naval firm called Gieve. Founder of Naval Tailoring firm Gieve that is now Gieve & Hawkes of Portsmouth. The 850-ton luxury was one of the largest to take part in the rescue at Dunkirk. Captain West served on board as navigator and this magnificent yacht and her gallant crewmembers safely brought back almost 2000 troops to Dover. Captain West was relieved at Dover and the yacht returned to the beaches and striking a mine, many of her brave crewmembers were killed and many were injured including the late Jack Wash of Tollesbury, a serving sailorman. His heroic father, a Tollesbury mariner, is mentioned in my works in 1926 MY Media story.

My late uncle Harold Stroud was born in Whitstable on the 31st January 1904, he sadly died on the 6th April 1964 at his Artic Road home, Cowes, Isle of Wight. Uncle was indeed the 1st mate on board the RRC Britannia 1931-1936, having five fisherman/yachtsman brothers. My uncle Harold being RNVR was soon called by the admiralty to serve his country and whilst serving on board one of Everard's fine ships at the start of the War he was very much involved with rescue operation on board HMS Gieve. His brother Fred Stroud RN perished at Iceland on a mission and was buried with full naval honours. When my uncle and his gallant crewmembers rescued some of the crew from on board they were covered in blood. They laid the men out upon the hatches on board ship and two of them rescued were his own two brothers, Albert Stroud who was the serving boatswain, having two broken legs and his brother, Jack Stroud, who was badly injured. Most sadly Jack and his lady wife lost a baby daughter around the same time. My good neighbour, Mr. Stan Sparkes aged 85 years, was indeed a full sergeant, a regular soldier in the guards at the downfall of Dunkirk. He was one of the many many soldiers who boarded a ship in Dunkirk harbour named SS Dan MackCree. Whilst serving at Normandy 6th June 1944 Stan was one of the four man crew serving a Bren gun carrier with, sorrow a German Commandant cornered, the small Bren gun carrier then turned and faced the crew with his large German tank, he then smiled, as much as to say we have you beaten. Stan was the only survivor. The youngest soldier was only 18 years old. Stan's three comrades were all killed as they sat like sitting ducks. Stan was severely injured at a place named Falais Gap 6th June 1944. After the war had gladly ended Stan spent many years serving on the Brightlingsea ambulance service with his close friend of late, also an Army man, Mr. Peter Dumbar. He was a most jovial man whom I often took fishing in my boat. Mr. Stan Sparkes and his wife Mrs. Peggy Sparkes have been our respected neighbours for over 44 years. A world record with no cross words. There are still a few men who served pre and post war on board the large sized luxury yachts but we are one and all getting on in years. But just recently, May 2000, with my friend Kenneth Wheeler it was nice to meet in the Royal British Legion at Tollesbury, Sailorman Mr. Raymond Harris and fellow members. Mr. Harris, a 1939-serving crewmember on board MY St. Modwin also served a total of 40 years as Parade Marshall of the Royal British Legion. The captain on board MY St. Modwin in 1939 was the late captain Joe Major of Brightlingsea and the 1st mate was the late captain Fred Rice of Tollesbury who was a lieutenant commander RN during the 2nd World War. A quiet gentleman whom I myself had sailed with to the Mediterranean during the 1950's when Mr. Rice joined MY Virginia RYS owned by late gentleman Lord Viscount Camrose who died in June 1954. Mr. Rice served as 1st officer for one season. The late captain Edward Pitt DSM was our good boatswain 2nd mate, a man I greatly admired and respected having sailed myself yachting with for seven years. He was always proud of being Wivenhoe born and bred. He resided in Southampton and lost two brothers during the 1st World War, John and Arthur Pitt. Mr. Pitt had served on board SY Sapphire II for 15 years pre 2nd World War as boatswain's mate. My own maritime father served and sailed on board for 7 seasons. Back to MY St. Modwin owner Colonel Gretton MP (1939) for Staffordshire, owner of Bass Breweries.

Late sailorman Mr. Charles Branch was a serving crewmember on board St Modwin in 1939 and being RNVR he was picked up by the Admiralty on the 3rd day of war Charlie had been a shipmate of my maritime father on board Sunbeam II, owned by gentleman Lord Runciman, Director of shipping line. Sunbeam II this 1936 yachting season had raced amongst the tall ships around the Islands in Canada. Late George Howelett served on board as focsle cook SY Sapphire in 1930's and SY St. Modwin in 1939. He had also sailed the world on board the 500-ton schooner Kallisto in 1925 with my maritime father and local shipmates. They are all named within the JJ collection. Mariners of West Mersea also served on board SY St. Modwin in 1939. Serving crewmember Mr. Peter Hills, yachtsman, coasting master and retired Trinity House pilot serving 34 years. He was a friend of Darby Stebbens. Peter mastered Everard's coasters, MV Capacity and MV Watermeet and he sailed on board Quenronald with fellow sailing barge skippers, late Fred Scales and late Fred Morgan. Shipmate Jack Wash of Tollesbury and Jack Stroud of Whitstable had both been serving seamen on board HMS Gieve May 29th 1940 and sailorman Jack Wash was sadly called to higher circles aged 60 years on June 6th when he most sadly died some time ago in the Royal British Legion at Tollesbury. His shipmate and sailorman friend Jack Stroud near Christmas in 1998, was heading for home after leaving the yacht club at the Hythe Southampton and most sadly crashed his car and he was killed. Like all his brothers they were all A1 sailormen, and Jack had skippered late gentleman Sir Phillip Hunlokes private yacht. Sir Phillip, being HM King George's sailing master on board the RRC Britannia. My uncle, Harold Stroud being 1st mate, as stated 1931-36.

On Saturday 27th May 2000 it was great for my friend Ken Wheeler and I to visit a fabulous riverside view, Heybridge Basin. We much enjoyed our meal in the riverside restaurant and having a friendly yarn with two pleasant lady members of staff and also gentleman artist Mr. Mike Lang, of Watercolour Workshops. All levels catered for. A friendly lady and gentleman also having lunch, well worthy of a mention, Mr. Herbert White RN 2nd World War, a leading seaman on board HMS Kent commanded by captain Abel Smith, a cousin of HM our Queen. HMS Kent carried 850 serving officers and ratings and was much involved sailing to Murmansk. She was also involved with tracking down the gigantic battleship Turpitz which was finally destroyed by British aircraft in the Norwegian fjords where, I am told the sea ran red with blood. Like our own Forces in war, all being some mother's sons. Mr. White was amazed when I said that on board MY Virginia RYS during the summer months in 1951, the late Duke of Westminster chartered this magnificent luxury yacht owned by the late Lord Viscount Camrose, who died in June 1954. We cruised through the magnificent scenery of the Norwegian fjords lying mostly as far North as Bossekop, which was where the Turpitz would hide out. A Norwegian salvage company was working on Turpitz when we sailed past. The Duke of Westminster spent most nights salmon fishing when we anchored up in the land of the midnight sun. All our crewmembers received a months wages as a present at the end of the charter, plus a large sized salmon per man. Our gentleman 2nd steward, Mr. Cyril Lake, aged 83 years, had served on board the late Viscount Lord Camrose's luxury yachts for many years and Cyril and I still correspond for old times sake. His father, a first class chef, was still preparing food for Lord Camrose until God's calling in June 1954. Recently, before boarding the bus to return home from Heybridge Basin, it is indeed a magnificent journey through unspoilt country with enjoyable birds and wildlife. Just by chance, Ken and I met Mr. Darby Stebbens and his kind lady wife, Janet. His father was indeed almost a 45-year serving Trinity House Pilot and certainly a most heroic mariner and lifesaver. I knew and respected this happy go lucky sailorman from my own seafaring career and involvement with the many ships laying in the river Blackwater in 1957. Thirty-two ships to be precise, tankers and cargo ships of which Mr. Stebbens was often the pilot on board.

HMS Marlborough tragedy November 1924. Sailorman Arthur Dowsett of Heybridge held a strong premonition that this would be his last voyage. He kissed his treasured mother farewell and gave his youngest brother a shilling (5p). He said to Arthur 'Do you want me to bring you some change?' 'No,' said Arthur 'I shall not be needing any money for a long time.' The late Mr. Don Drake of Brightlingsea was due to join these qualified mariners for just the run job from Portsmouth to Heybridge Basin but the late Mr. Gray of Maldon, owner of the yacht Raven, wished to stay on his yacht for a few days. Mr. Drake had a lucky escape. After the tragedy he started his own local fish trade for many a year. It blew half a gale when HMS Marlborough left Portsmouth and being well open above the waterline the seams were open.

Myself as a young lad and living next door to Mrs. Wheeler, known to my late brother Alfred and I as Granny Annie Wheeler. Come November 19th 1944 this quiet lady needed no telling that her son, Ernest who had joined the world famous racing schooner Westward as the ship's carpenter in 1926 under the command of the late Captains Alf Diaper, senior and junior of the River Itchen. Late William Aldous of local served as 1st mate for 26 years being a most supreme sailorman on board Shamrocks, White Heather and mate of Navahoe in 1908. Chippy Ernest Wheeler lived on board schooner Westward, whilst working ashore on Admiralty war work at Dartmouth. On a Sunday night, 19th November 1944 whilst rowing back to board Westward in a strong gale of wind along with the racing yacht's regular boatswain, Mr. Walter Saunders of Portsmouth. They both perished saving fellow man. On the Monday morning I went round to help my mother to fill the old water buckets from the stanchion pipe taps and we, one and all, had in those days the old outdoor Palace of Varieties! Granny Wheeler came out at 8.30am for her usual yarn. Numbers at 15 and 11, Nelson Street, local and said to my mother that God and her husband, Captain Frederick had paid her a special visit and told her not to worry as he would look after her only son alright and also of boatswain Mr. W. Saunders. Their bodies were laid to rest quite near to the Naval Cemetery at Dartmouth. My friend's brother, Arthur Wheeler aged 81, years who served RN during the 2nd World War spent a great deal of his time, from the age of 4 years living with Granny Annie Wheeler, and also time with Mr. and Mrs. Jack and Mary Ellis at their lovely riverside home, of which many a story of the sea is still untold from the mariners who used the Inn, once known as the Live & Let Live. Locally known as the Anchorage at Heybridge Basin being the lovely warm and friendly home of Mr. and Mrs. Darby and Janet Stebbens who showed Ken and I much kindness. Mr. Jack Stebbens and his lady wife were indeed Darby's most loveable uncle and auntie and it broke many a heart within the family when Mr. Jack Ellis left his warm home, Anchorage, on a bitter cold night on February 5th 1942, aged 70 years, to walk down and religiously check the lock gates. He accidentally slipped on some ice and into the lock and sadly he drowned. The following day the water was pumped out and his body was recovered. This also broke Granny Wheeler's heart having lost five members of the Wheeler family who had all drowned at sea. Not only had Mr. Cecil Stebbens, being a life saver on board the old HMS Marlborough, ex HMS Vernon, he once more became a hero overnight when saving a little 5 year old girl from drowning. In recognition of his action in jumping into the cold water of the River Crouch and Burnham, May 2nd Cecil Leslie Stebbens who was standing on the quay at Burnham and spotted a small child in the river. Without hesitation he took off his Trinity House pilot jacket and hat and swam out 12 yards to the child, caught hold of her and brought her to safety. The Mayor congratulated him for his prompt action and he was presented with the Royal Humane Societies Testimonial by the Mayor Alderman E. C, Dines JP at Maldon Court 8th September 1953. Trinity House pilot and fisherman Mr. Cecil Stebbens with a family tradition following of 145 years prestige. He himself completed almost 45 years loyal service. At one stage he was mate on board the old sailing barge Shamrock which struck an obscure object out through the Raisen Sands, the skipper, mate, boy and dog were saved and the crew rowed all the way back to Burnham. Dogs on board barges were most vital and served as a radar system for during fog they would communicate with other dogs on shore and the brilliant old sailing masters would know their position. Mr. Cecil Stebbens retired in 1972 and was called to higher circles in March 1973 aged 71 years. God bless his memory, gone but not forgotten. Mr. Darby Stebbens, being a retired fisherman who followed a family tradition with a love of the sea and of his father the same as his kind lady wife Janet. She loved fishing with her hard working seafarer late husband, Darby. Being a powerful man in his prime, and a good swimmer often towed barges and yachts with his family vessel in and out of Maldon and Heybridge. After the 2nd World War their family fishing boat was an ex Air Sea Rescue Craft renamed FV Bluebird. During the 2nd World War her name was RAF Allenby, she was 38 feet in length, 2 feet 6 inches draft. She could enter into shallow water for rescue and fishing. Darby earned a good livelihood when very often alone, night time otter trawling, and this was all handraulic, pulling in his harvest from the sea by hand.

Maldon

Home of many of the well preserved lovely old working barges with still many untold stories to tell. Within the JJ collection log-books, chronicles, photographs and household names awaiting honest publication. On behalf of my friend Ken and I we would like to express in this story our sincere appreciation to one and all that have made this very special maritime story/history book possible. Also our gratitude is expressed in full to lady Ann and husband Norrie, Mr. and Mrs. Tomlinson. Ann, Lady Commodore of the Little Ships Club at Maldon, and all club members, proud owners of their little ships. Owners with a love of the sea. Respect and kindness, which is always shown on our visit to the Little Ships Club towards the JJ lifetime's recordings. Most sacred to all their memory, may God bless you one and all.

I, John A. Jefferies, maritime historian would like to end my short story of the sea by paying homage to a young man who sacrificed his young life, aged 42 years, to do his utmost to save a young girl from drowning. On behalf of my wife Jean, our hearts go out to David's mother and his respected family members, and his lady friend. Brave Mr. David Brett with a heart of gold was a friend of my son Dereck, and he joined us in the festivities of Dereck's birthday party held at Dovercourt on 29th April 2000. He was a much-loved son and was hero-worshiped by his mother. David became a hero overnight.

My story is of the cruel sea and I pray to God that David's good name can go down in history for the most brave courageous and gallant young man that he was. No man could have greater love, than to sacrifice his life for fellow human beings.

God bless all their memory within my works for those in peril on the sea.

Captain Charles Pitt, Maritime at the wheel of S.Y. "Medea".
Born in 1874 Grandson of ship owner and Victuallen of East Donyland.
Pictured after the tragedy of the loss of Captain Rice on his last voyage serving as Chief Officer in the Gulf of Lyons in 1926.

Previously Captain Pitt served as Commander RNR Western approaches 1914-18 followed by being Chief Officer of C.S. Guardian when laying the first transatlantic telegraph cable into S. America (1920).

Captain Pitt and Captain Rice were both exemplary Mariners.

OUR MARITIME HERITAGE AND THE FAMOUS SHAMROCK V 1930 AMERICA'S CUP CHALLENGE.

Captain Thomas and Captain Paul - Shamrock V.
The damage encountered on homeward passage from U.S.A. 1930 on the run back to England.

Shamrock IV Crew, 1914.
The crew was mastered by Captain Albert Turner (Wivenhoe), First Mate Captain Ned Heard (Tollesbury).
W. Hazelton, W. Riley, R. Howe, A. Bowles and brothers J. & J. Gilby serving officers, all known by J.J.

Enclosed are the photographs of our forgotten masters, navigators and mariners. Left to right on board Shamrock IV, depicted in photograph (above) are Captains Thomas and Paul who were navigating officers at that time. Much damage was encountered on the homeward voyage to England due to heavy seas. On the outward passage Captain Durrum of Southampton who was in command of the fabulous steam yacht S.Y. Albion. The famous Captain Ned Heard together with his gallant crew, on the outward voyage to America were missing for five whole days. This was never reported. Captain Durrum steamed 800 nautical miles in search of Shamrock V until contact was made off the Azores. The son of Captain Ned Heard, Ted Heard Junior, who was a serving crew member, sadly passed away at the grand old age of ninety three, on the seventeenth of February 1999. Also, my shipmate and friend Dan Mutton of Port Isaac, who passed away, at the grand old age of ninety five, on the 25th November 1995. Dan served Shamrock V as boatswain in 1930. I have lived with this knowledge for many years.

During the outward voyage to the USA a heavy sea boarded and filled the lifeboat to the gunnels. Crew member, Slim Pengelly of Looe in Cornwall, was tragically killed in a motorcycle accident in Gosport High Street after his safe return from the USA in 1937. He had said to Frank Paddy of Plymouth "Look the bloody lifeboat is waterlogged." Frank Paddy soon replied, with a sense of good humour. "Yes, you would be the first to shit blue lights if we should need it."

Shamrock V crew members from 1930, who have all been named in my recordings, returned home from the USA on board S.S. Coronia. Shamrock V was returned to England by navigators Captains Thomas and Paul, and good American Yachtsmen, were the run crew for the voyage home. They encountered much damage on board from the heavy Atlantic Seas late at the end of the yachting season.

F. Banks *Capt. Sycamore* *Sir T. Lipton* *Mr G. L. Watson* *G. Biffen*
Chief Steward *Commander* *Designer* *Chief Officer*

The Owner, Designer, Commander, Officers and Crew of Shamrock II
(from a photograph by W. Blain, Dumbarton)

SACRED TO THEIR MEMORY
1930 SHAMROCK V SERVING CREW MEMBERS

1930 Maritime Heritage and The Last Attempt of Sir Thomas Lipton Making His Final Challenge for the America's Cup

I must add that this gentleman was respected throughout the world and also by his gallant crew members for being the worlds greatest sportsman and loser. He was indeed a gentleman. I am proud of the fact that the world famous Captain Robert Wringe, who commanded over the many yachting seasons, Shamrocks 1, 2 and 3 was, my great uncle. He died at his Sandy Hook home in Brightlingsea on 14th February 1924 aged 64 years.

The mariners depicted on this photograph were the last serving crew members who so gallantly tried on the fifth attempt to regain the America's Cup to our shores as stated above. After leaving the Azores the first mate, Lemon Cranfield of Rowhedge, was taken ill and he was transferred to the S.Y. Albion which was under the command of Captain Durrum of Southampton. With regret, Mr. Cranfield took no active part as the serving 1st mate for the challenge. Sailorman Bert French, a native of West Mersea who was the serving 2nd mate on board Shamrock V took over the mates position. Late Charles Pewter of Tollesbury, who was the serving chief steward on board S.Y. Albion nursed Mr.Cranfield back to health. After the America's Cup series, the crew of Shamrock V sailed back to England from America on board S.S. Coronia. Shamrock V crew list from the 1930 challenge is as follows:-

My friend, the late Dan Mutton who was called to rest 25th November 1995 aged 95 years, served as boatswain, unfortunately he is not included in the photograph. The Stroud brother's, Whitstable in Kent, yachtsmen who numbered seven in all, had also served King and Country at sea during the 2nd World War. The late Harold Stroud, whom I am proud to claim as my uncle. He served the R.R.C. Brittania as 1st mate 1931-36.

1930 Shamrock V - serving crew (from left to right)

Back Row - C. Dan (Wivenhoe), T. Cudmore (W. Mersea), S. Stroud (Whitstable), L. Cranfield (Rowhedge), Capt. E. Heard (Tollesbury), B. French (W. Mersea), A. Stroud (Whitstable), C. Heard (Tollesbury), C. Hillard (Wivenhoe).

Middle Row - J. Sergeant (Looe), J. Ugloe (Looe), W. Braddick (Brixham), J. Gempton (Brixham), W. Wilkinson (Tollesbury), S. Harman 'Sucky' (Whitstable).

Front Row: D. Howard (W. Mersea), T. Heard-jnr (Tollesbury), A.J. Pengelly B.E.M. (Looe), H. German (Brixham), F. Paddy.

Not in photograph - C. Stokes, 17th sailorman (Tollesbury), D. Mutton (Port Isacc) and Sailorman late Hector Frost of Tollesbury. It is believed that late boatswain Dan Mutton took this photograph.

Shamrock V - Trip Across Atlantic.

Record of entries in Log Book by A.J. Pengelly B.E.M. of Looe, Cornwall.

This log was kept and recorded by late sailorman A.J. Pengelly B.E.M. of Looe. This was supplied "with my kindest wishes to JJ historian" from Mr Terry Pengelly, mariner of Looe son of A.J. Pengelly.

Slipped our moorings and left Gosport on July 19th at 11am. Cleared the harbour amid much cheering and blowing of sirens. Outside we adjusted compasses. Later we brought up off Ryde as there was a strong wind through the Needles. In the evening got anchor and towed behind Erin as far as Jack in the Basket, that is the entrance to Solent waters, and laid there until early morning.

Sunday 20th - Got underway at 5am and towed clear of the Wight, shaped course down Channel, still behind Erin. Set mizzen and jib to keep her steady with a strong wind south west, kept going until we reached Start Point. The wind freshened and being late afternoon decided to run back to Brixham to shelter for the night. Dropped anchor 6pm, raining and blowing hard. A Government trawler sent aboard the Sunday papers so the rest of the evening was spent reading.

Monday 21st - Hauled up anchor, took towline aboard and left Brixham at 5am opened out the Start Point. Wind Nor West moderate, with a heavy swell from the westward. 10am reefed trysail, set mizzen and jib. Punched down channel past the Eddystone, and was abreast of Lizard at 3pm. Shook out reef in trysail, slipped tow rope and with a fresh wind W.N.W. shaped course W.b.S. 3/4S in a few hours the English shore was lost to sight.

Tuesday 22nd - 4am. Wind moderate N. Sea going down, set mizzen staysail. 6am got it off her again rolling very heavy the running gear chafing to pieces, put parcelling on everything movable, signalled Erin to pick us up, she replied we must keep going while we have a breeze. So with light wind N.E. set squaresail and lowered trysail and staysail steering W.b.S. 1/4s. Later wind draws easterly light. Lowers square sail, sets trysail and staysail still rolling heavy. Takes towline aboard and makes good progress all day. 12pm wind makes N.b.W. squally.

Wednesday 23rd - Strong wind, battened down fore and aft, heavy squalls. 8am wind drops lighter, noon opens up hatches. Tramp speaks to us at 10am wished us good luck and bon voyage, wind keeps light all day, at midnight it is calm.

Thursday 24th - Sky alters fast and a strong wind makes from the south west, on goes the hatches again the sea is quickly making up, sets trysail reefed, lowers mizzen and are forced to slip towrope. Blows hard, 4pm wind veers S.S.W. with hard squalls, very uncomfortable below, battenen down, having meals amid ships on the floor, banging hard, can't get any sleep, some in the sail bins amid ships and some down aft cannot go in the forecastle to sleep. What a night. Erin spoke to us 8pm, gave us some news. Midnight still blowing with heavy rain squalls, wind breaks us off a little. The Erin keeps jogging on our port quarter, more heavy rain, wind veered to west, loses sight of escort.

Friday 25th - 7am. Wind dropping sets small staysail, still plenty of sea. 9am shakes out reef in trysail, wind still W. and the Erin is nowhere to be seen after disappearing like the Phantom ship of old. Sky clears away, wind drops light and it smoothes fine, sets big staysail to dry off. 8pm resets small staysail, stowing large one below.

Saturday 26th - 4am. Wind keeps light westerly. At 10am veers S.W. still fine. 3pm fog sets in and remains all through the night.

Sunday 27th - 4am. Wind light W. Sky clears at noon, the wind shifts to N.W., light airs sets bowspit spinnaker, later draws easterly with rain. 6pm wind N.E. rain. Got spinnaker down set square sail and with a nice breeze ran at a good pace all night.

Monday 28th - 8am. Wind still aft, noon lower square sail and set bowspit spinnaker and mizzen staysail, wind light South East. 6pm. Set jib and staysail and trysail and lowered spinnaker, wind still the same way, light, keeping so all night.

Tuesday 29th - 4am. Wind same. 6am, set third jib. 11am wind light W. Sights the Azores early morning and draws abreast of Tereyra Island 8am to windward of us (midnight wind W.S.W. all hands does their washing and dries up all wet gear and clothing).

Wednesday 30th - 8am. Got headsails down and set bowspit spinnaker, later decided to change it so down with it. Set big staysail and third jib and came close hauled on the wind to make our port of call which we had in sight at noon. Entering Fayal harbour 3pm, we found the Erin had arrived 10am the same morning after having spent five days looking for us in vain. Clear up decks and 6pm starboard watch ashore.

Thursday 31st - Varnish through. 2pm, port watch ashore for two hours. 5pm left Fayal, took towline aboard at 7pm, wind N. fresh with long ground swell, kept steady pace all night.

Friday 1st August - 4am. Wind dropping, set trysail double reefed. 8am. Wind light N. Noon very fine sea going down. 4pm. Lovely weather, lowers trysail. Midnight wind moderate W.

Saturday 2nd - 8am. Wind W. all day moderate, got plenty of sleep in.

Sunday 3rd - 5.30am. Mate went sick, signalled Erin who launched boat and took him back for medical attention where he remained the rest of the trip. A large whale rose on our starboard quarter. Wind N.W.

Monday 4th - 4am. Set trysail, mizzen and jib, rolling heavy, wind drawing more from the westward. 8am. Shook one reef out of trysail, set staysail and slipped our towrope. Noon, wind moderates. 4am. Wind and sea going down. 6pm. Erin spoke to us in tow again and kept on our course with a light wind ahead.

Wednesday 6th - 4am. Wind freshening. 8am. Erin keeps away four points for us to make better weather of it, with the wind on the port bow more sea making. Noon. Nasty sea for this little ship. 4pm. Seems a little finer. Midnight wind back W.S.W. freshening.

Thursday 7th - 4am. Strong wind and nasty sea making from south west. Noon. Hard wind and heavy sea. A good sea boat this but mast looks shaky, "never ought to have come to sea with it". Most everybody fed up. 4pm no change. 8pm. Looks awful, strong W.S.W. Midnight. Repaired port swinging strut stay, still blowing hard. Very little sleep to be had.

Friday 8th - 4am. Wind coming up in squalls with enough rain to knock one flat, "some one or other must have killed a cat!!!" 8am. More squalls can't look to winard in them, not a wink of sleep to get anywhere. Everything wet through, "what a life". Carries away flag halyards and port topping lift on square sail yard. Noon. A little better weather. 4pm. Think it's moderating a bit. 6pm. Rolling nearly upside down. 8pm. Wind veered to W.N.W. finer sea, going down. Midnight fine with bright moonlight, what a contrast!

Saturday 9th - 4am. Making good progress, light wind N.W. 9.30am. Erin stopped and sent aboard fresh stores, reports mate's improvement, also they are running short of coal. If we get many more strong head winds she will have to slip us and make the best of it on our own to let her go to the nearest port for bunkers. Midday. Wind logging nine, all day repaired port lift and dried up all damp gear. 8pm. Breeze making S.W. Midnight. Wind freshening, set reefed trysail.

Sunday 10th - 4am. Wind strong S.W. 8am. Same. Noon. Still strong wind but not a lot of sea. 4pm. Only 496 miles to do, spirits rise, wind and sea more abeam. Not looking too bad, logging a steady nine, if we can keep this up shall be in by Wednesday. 6pm. Have lowered trysail, got tired of slacking sheet off while Erin cleans fires. This our fourth Sunday out, we are all getting heartily fed up, can't get a decent nap when we are battened down, and we have to be as soon as there is a hat full of wind. Midnight. Strong hard wind and heavy sea from S.W.

Monday 11th - 4am. Rotten morning, hard and rolling like a barrel. 8am. Had one unlucky sea break aboard which filled the lifeboat up and cockpit, shan't want many more like that before something will be shifting. 8am. Never known her to roll so much. Man at the wheel has to have lashing around him, tried to get breakfast, plates running all over the floor, the atmosphere below is very bad, hot and damp, everything wet through. Have not been forard for three nights. Below, the only one there is the cook, and he has to sit on the floor to watch his stoves cooking. We have been lucky to get anything cooked some days. Have had very hard rain squalls but they have brought a little finer weather. 1.30pm. An American steam yacht spoke to us. 4pm. Still rolling but wind dropped and sea going down. 4.30pm. Tea time, tinned pilchards on the floor of the mess room waiting to be dished out. A sea breaks aboard, some of it happens to find it's way down the opened skylight over the mess room, "exit pilchards from tins", we have a busy time scraping them off the floor. "What a life" fishing on the mess room floor. 6pm. No wind, looks like rain. Midnight Breeze and rain from N.E.

Tuesday 12th - 2am. Wind light N.W. continuing until 4pm. when it freshened a little dropping at midnight.

Wednesday 13th - 4am. Calm, going a good pace. They are waking her up in the Erin's stockhold, past Nantucket, early morning. Getting close to the American coast now. Noon. We are being greeted by fast launches from New London. Enters the harbour with a strong escort of yachts and Government boats, plenty of cameramen taking movies. Well, here we are in America and glad to have got here too. Everybody seems to want Shamrock to win the cup and we'll see she does, too.

History.

First Cup Race August 22nd, 1851. Yacht American 170 ton, from Cowes around Isle of Wight, 15 Challengers with Shamrock V. First Shamrock was in 1899. Deed of Gift of America's Cup by George Shaylor 1857 to be raced by sloops of not less than 65ft. water line. Ten months notice of challenge.

Preparations for Cup Races

Sept 5th - Left Newport for day's sail 10.30am, returned 5pm, wind S.S.E. moderate, unbent No.1 mainsail.

Sept 6th - Bent No.2 mainsail. Went for a trial spin. Returned 4pm, unbent mainsail.

Sept 7th - Varnish through the ship, afternoon off, first spell since we arrived in America.

Sept 8th - Ship dry docked to clean the bottom. Sand papered mast and top mast. Varnished it after dinner.

Sept 9th - Cleaned off ship's topsides with sandpaper.

Sept 10th - Varnished the launch out.

Sept 11th - Left dock, put to moorings, bent No.3 mainsail. After dinner went for a sail. Did not stop out, too much wind.

Sept 12th - Set jib and staysail and reefed the mainsail. Went to dinner. After, went for a sail, passed close to H.M.S. Halltroppe whose crew gave us a hearty cheer. Returned at 3.30pm. Everyone now anxiously waiting for the first day of the big races.

First Day of Races

Sept 13th - 9am. Left the moorings amid much cheering and blowing of hooters and sirens. Arrived at the starting line which was nine miles from land. Starting time 11.50am was delayed owing to lightness of wind. Starts off at 1pm with a spinnaker run. Enterprise having the best of the start, she keeps her lead and reaches the lea mark two minutes ahead of Shamrock. Coming back close hauled she gains ½ minute finishing 2½ minutes ahead.

Sept 14th - General clean up of ship doing odd jobs. Removed 1 ton of lead.

Sept 15th - 2nd race. Started at 11.50am with a ten mile beat to windward, 10 mile reach and 10 mile run, weather fine. Had a splendid weather start but the Enterprise soon shows her superiority in speed by beating us 6 minutes to the first mark, increasing her lead to nine minutes to second mark, half minute on the lap home beating us easily by 9½ minutes. Gets moored and takes out No.2 mainsail. Everybody losing heart in the Shamrock, can see now we are out on a hopeless task, too big, and odds against us, puts the lead in again.

Sept 16th - Race Postponed owing to fog. Bends No. 3 mainsail.

Sept 17th - Started at 11.50am with a 15 mile beat to windward, had another lovely start crossing the line with Enterprise under our lee, both on starboard tack. After a few minutes, Enterprise tacks, we immediately do the same, we are still on his weather bow. After five minutes tacked again, main halyards carried away, so we are out of it again. Enterprise carries on to win her third race. Rather unlucky but were badly beaten at the time. Returned to harbour, rove off new main halyards all ready for tomorrow's races.

Sept 18th - Started off at 11.50am, both being on the line in good time. Our first lap was 10 miles to windward and it was not long before Enterprise was well in the lead, beating us by 9½ minutes to the first mark. Our next being a 10 mile reach which we picked up two minutes on her and on the last lap a broad reach we picked up another 2½ minutes making it 4½ minutes. Enterprise finished five minutes ahead of us, so that ended the series of races for the cup 1930.

THE AMERICAN CUP DEFENDER - AND A BEAUTY

Harold S. Vanderbilt's "Ranger," Her soaring white sails filled with sunlight and wind;
She's flirted her heals at all competitors and until they're shown better -
Mr Vanderbilt and his supporters will declare she's the swiftest racing yacht ever built.

Picture and words from the Sunday Mirror.

ENDEAVOUR

Maritime - Sacred to their memory

By J. A. Jefferies - Author, retired Mariner, Maritime Historian

1937 Endeavour Crew Members. Back row left to right.

Late Jim Mussett (West Mersea), Harry German (Brixham), Robert Parker (River Itchen), Jim Stubbins (had 9 children), Neville Gurton (Tollesbury), Late Jim Cann (Port Isaac), Duncan Curry (Scotland), Jack Gempton, mate (Brixham), Harry Jumbo Randall (Hythe), Bill Lewis (Tollesbury), Captain Ned Heard (Tollesbury), Walter Pengally (Looe), Late Dan Mutton (Port Isaac), Late Cyril Coates (Tollesbury), Jack Sergeant (Looe), Len Pengally (Looe), Joe Ugloc (Looe), Captain Abrams, superb navigator square rigged sailorman, Horace Chatteron (Tollesbury), Ted Heard jnr. (Tollesbury). Jack Frost transferred to Endeavour X from M.Y. Phillante (Tollesbury). The photograph was taken by a crew member.

1937 - 2006 (69 years).

As we have now reached October 2006 it is sixty-nine years since the world famous America's cup challengers Endeavour II and Endeavour, trial horse, returned home to Gosport to a heroes welcome. The Lutine Bell had been rung at Lloyds, this causing grave concern for many families with loved ones who were serving onboard these gigantic racing machines, having been built by the best method of all - the human hand. By A1 craftsmen and tradesmen of Camper and Nicholsons Gosport, highly respected and world renowned for their first class workmanship and design. As I sailed through life kind words were always exchanged with Gentleman Mr. Charles Nicholson of Camper and Nicholsons, Northam and also Gentleman Mr Peter Nicholson during my yachting career.

So to continue with my life happenings, and knowing personally many of the Masters and the mariners of Great Britain, plus sailing with and befriending good sailor men and mariners who had sailed on board many famous yachts, including Endeavours. On October 1st 1937 arriving into Gosport with all ships sirens sounding, a greeting from the public and late city mayor, Major Graham C.F.O. afforded the returning crew members a heroes welcome, and a civic reception had been arranged. However, with the greatest respects this extremely kind gesture was declined by the late Captain Ned Heard of Tollesbury, the home of many a brilliant yacht master and sailor man. All that Captain Heard, along with his gallant crew members, wished to do was to return home to their native village of Tollesbury and their loved ones who for many days had prayed for all their safety during the ordeal of the typhoon. I had the honour and privilege of knowing Captain Ned Heard from my youth and manhood days, from prior to the second world war when the good mariners of Tollesbury made their hard earned living in their fishing vessels during the bitter cold winter months, and serving on world famous yachts with equally famous yacht owners.

Photograph taken Rhode Island USA.
Standing on deck in white shirt the late Wally Day of Southampton, A1 Sailorman, and Captain Williams, right hand man. Kneeling down 2nd mate Bill Taw. R.I. shipmate of my maritime father in 1926 serving and racing on board the famous 24 metre racing cruiser Lulworth. A daughter of Bill, along with her pleasant husband, retired from their Woolston, Southampton shoe shop business, being near to treasured memories of the lovely old steam floating bridge, we often met and yarned of bygone days. Also in photograph Sailorman Phil William,s cousin Beth, and World famous Captain G. Williams.

Rhode Island USA.
Standing on deck late sailorman friend who was called to higher circles summer 1985 aged 78 years. On right of sailorman Mr. Phil Williams this lady was his cousin Beth who resided at Rhode Island and was also cousin to the world famous Captain George Williams who was buried at sea 150 miles West of the Azores 22nd September 1937 aged 58 years.

Endeavour II was under the command of world famous sailing master Captain G. Williams of Hamble river, being one of six sailor men brothers. My father had sailed with Captain Billy Williams on board the racing yacht Susanna when sadly, on a night passage, a Brightlingsea yachtsman (name withheld) hung himself upon the mast.

Sailor man supreme, the late Phil Williams, along with his lady wife Mrs. Vera Williams, a most kind lady aged 95 years in 1997 whom it was indeed my pleasure to visit along with members of her family. For several years Mr. and Mrs. Williams resided at the fabulous Royal British Legion flats overlooking the Solent river at Netley. Endeavour II sailorman Phil, had been shipmate to my late uncle Albert Jefferies in 1930 when the schooner Xarifa, owned by the late gentleman Mr. Singer, the yacht was commanded by Captain Dickerson of Warsash, 1st mate the late Bert Gladdin of Cowes, Isle of Wight, when Xarifa came out of Archashan in the Bay of Biscay and went missing for ten whole days. This made headline stories in the News of the World for two weeks running. (The full facts and all photographs are contained within my main stories, which are awaiting honest sponsorship for publication). Sailor man Mr. Phil Williams would call me 'Mr. Bricklesea' during my visits and would say to me "write it all down my boy. The stories of us crew members are forgotten and should be told, if not for my sake but for the sake of families and humanities". Sailor man Phil Williams was called to rest in the early summer of 1985 aged 78 and I did write it all down, thank God, including recording all household names and details in every photograph. So to continue with Phil's story. "A most sad day in our lives aboard Endeavour II after many famous yachts attempted to regain America's cup to our shores, tragedy happened on board the ocean racer Endeavour II the challenger, but the Ranger (the American entry) retained the cup for America.

Sailorman Phil Williams and Author J.J. in nautical conversation during one of my visits to his warm and friendly home, R.B.L. flats Netley. It was a joy to visit Mr. Williams and his lady wife Mrs.Vera Williams. Sailorman Phil was called to higher circles aged 78 early in the summer of 1985.

Endeavour II upon the end of her long towrope five days out from Rhode Island Radio W/T from Block Island weather station advised a typhoon was approaching at 106 m.p.h. During this Typhoon my Brother, Captain George Williams, sailing master, laid in his bunk in agony suffering untold pain with a bleeding ulcer whilst mountainous seas 16 feet high pounded over us. Sadly the challenger was being challenged with the yacht, master, officers, navigator and gallant crew all at the mercy of the most vicious seas. It was impossible for a boat to be lowered from the brand new motor yacht Phillante under the command of the late Captain McKillop, who was known and highly respected by John Jefferies. The following day a launch was lowered and boatswain Mack and two brave sailor men, along with Doctor P. Milligan, boarded Endeavour II risking their own lives in doing so. Upon examination of my brother a most critical situation was revealed and an S.O.S. was immediately sent out and was picked up by the French liner, S.S. Normandie, with which rendezvous was made at 00.10 hours the following day to transfer Captain Williams. The wind had slightly eased away with a heavy sea still running. Captain McKillop ordered boatswain Mack to lengthen the towrope and proceed towing at full speed. By now several crewmembers were able to stand on deck relieved at the passage of the storm. Captain McPhee, the brilliant navigator had sadly died on the outward passage and was laid to rest in American soil.

The challenger Endeavour II 1937 being challenged in Mid Atlantic. A few crew members could hardly stand on deck during the height of the storm

Right:
Standing on deck the late Mr. Frank Murdoch, stress strain winch and rigging world famous designer for Hawker Siddley. On right Captain McPhee the brilliant navigator who sadly died on board and was laid to rest on American soil.

Doctor P. Milligan on calling me below decks said with these kind words 'your brother is nearing the end of his life upon God's Earth', he died half an hour later. Not only had Endeavour II lost the challenge but the courageous crew members had lost their world famous Commander, and I had to announce to my loyal shipmates that their sailing master's life was over and that he had seen the harbour lights regretfully racing us home. Prior to God's calling, my brother asked me to pass him the ship's log book and he managed to scribble within the log 'these sailor men were all hand picked by myself, each and every man was trained to perfection. They did their utmost to regain the America's cup to our shores, no man could ask for more. God bless you one and all. Signed Captain George Williams Sailing Master Endeavour II.' He was buried at sea on the 22nd September 1937, 150 miles west of Azores.

Mid Atlantic 1937
Sir Thomas Sopwith, American cup challenger Endeavour II outward passage to America. The Belgian trawler Jon was much involved with towing.

Endeavour II in 1937 America's Cup Challenger
A fabulous photograph with the late Captain George Williams far left whom along with his A1 Sailorman, 1st mate and right hand man, the late Wally Day of Southampton, had trained each and every sailorman to perfection. Captain Williams worshipped his heroic crew members.

Here follow some household names of serving, brilliant sailor men who challenged on board Endeavour II 1937: The Late Wally Day, first mate, Southampton, late Bill Taw, second mate, Southampton, Jim Collier, Boatswain, Emsworth. Hector Frost, Tollesbury, F. Stoner, St. Ives. Dan Potter, Tollesbury. The late Bill Randall, Emsworth who died aged 80 years in 1980. The late 'Tooley' Alf Kennet, a most brilliant mastheadsman, Emsworth. A much loved family man. Whilst serving on board the lovely and restored to full glory, the fabulous J class Velsheda during the 1930's racing seasons, called out aloud to his brother Edward 'Bumper' Kennet, who was a serving crew member on board the J class Candida under the command of the late Captain Billy Randall of Emsworth, "you have a son, named Peter". Also serving seaman on board Endeavour II 1937 remembered were J. Dredge, E. Jones, Alec Mclean of the Outer Hebrides, Muller White, Gosport, late skipper Jim Slorance of Southampton. My father had sailed shipmates with some of these mariners and Jim Slorance and I had been shipmates on board M.Y. Virginia R.Y.S. Mediterranean cruising.

At the very young age of 18 Robert Parker of the river Itchen was the No. 2 mastheadsman serving on board Endeavour, under the command of Captain Ned Heard, and was standing on the deck during the height of the typhoon when a gigantic sea of 16 feet high knocked them both overboard. They were both very fortunate to be saved by the lifelines attached to their waists and also by the grace of God. A1 Sailor man rigger, Mr Robert Parker and his Lady Wife, I have made visits to their warm and friendly home.

Sailorman Supreme
Robert Parker
of the river Itchen,
Southampton.

The late Mrs. Isobel Parker of the river Itchen, mother of Robert, also made headline news in 1937 as she had a premonition. A robin had tapped upon her kitchen window and she had a very strong feeling all would be safe and well from the tempest

A fantastic live shot of Endeavour racing off Rhode Island USA.
Left: For'd Joe Ugloe of Looe, Cornwall.
Middle: Sailorman Robert Parker of the river Itchen, Mastheadsman No.2 at age 18 the youngest serving crew member.
Right: Sailorman Duncan Curry of Scotland No.1 Mastheadsman. A1 sailorman and greatly respected shipmate of Endeavour crew.

Six very smart seamen serving Endeavour ready for a run ashore. Rhode Island U.S.A.

From left to right:
1. The late Jim Mussett of West Mersea
2. Bill Lewis of Tollesbury
3. Jack Sergeant of Looe, Cornwall
4. Duncan Curry of Scotland
5. Jim Stubbins of Tollesbury (had 9 children) 6. Len Slim of Pengelly of Looe.

Sailor in vest - Harry German of Brixham

of the sea. On board Endeavour was sailor man the late Jim Mussett of West Mersea, who was called to rest on the 21st July 1997, he was also a great shipmate of my late uncle Harold Stroud serving on board the famous 24 metre racing cruiser Lulworth in 1927 under the command of the late captain Charles Bevis of the river Itchen. In the 1926 racing season whilst my father was a serving crew member winning more prize money whilst racing than taking wages.

My late uncle Harold Stroud, a most brilliant seaman, had served on board the royal racing cutter Britannia as 1st mate from 1931-36. Uncle was called to rest at his Arctic Road home Cowes, Isle of Wight. He was born on the 31st January 1904 and died on the 6th April 1964. He was one of six very popular yachting brothers of Whitsable, Kent. Two of his charming daughters, and of my mother's sister, therefore my cousins Eileen and Elizabeth reside in Eastleigh, Southampton, and I am pleased to report that we are good friends and communicate on a regular basis. On the 16th July 1987 Jim and Nancy Mussett and myself were kindly invited to, and made

Photograph of the Author taken in the Royal Southern Yacht Club at a press conference by kind permission of gentleman Commodore Mr. Grinyer 1989/90

It was taken upon my 60th birthday 15th July 1989, the day previous to Captain John Barrett USA leaving Southampton with his jovial crew members on the 16th July 1989 sailing for America with the fabulously restored to glory, Endeavour, the 1934 challenger, owned now by an American Lady Miss Myers who sadly was unwell during the time of the relaunching at the Hythe Side, Calshot, Southampton.

On the right world famous gentleman the late Mr. Frank Murdoch who had not heard tell of any of his gallant shipmates in all those years.

Part crew on board having a nautical yarn. All trained to perfection by Captain G. Williams Gentleman smoking pipe, late Mr. Frank Murdoch world famous Hawker Siddley winch, rigging, stress and strain expert.

most welcome at a press conference held at the Royal Southern Yacht club. It was great to have a nautical yarn with gentleman Mr. Arthur Nicholson and also Mr. Harry Spencer of Spencer Rigging Engineers, block makers, supreme craftsman and designers. I must also add that it is an honour for my friend Ken and I to always enjoy a visit to Mr. Spencer's rigging loft and we much enjoy his most humorous and jovial company over lunch at times. With the same welcome made whilst saying hello to the world famous maritime photographer Kenneth Beken and his staff in Cowes, Isle of Wight; close and loyal friends reside near and around the R.Y.S. with the late gentleman Mr. Jim Higgins and his lady wife Bonnie being head stewards of the R.Y.S. for eighteen years. Also close friends at this time, being relatives of gentleman Jim were Tex, his late wife Joy and Dee, both sisters of Bonnie. Jim was also the gentleman president of the Royal British Legion, Cowes, Isle of Wight. It was an honour for myself to have this gentleman and his family as loyal friends. Jim was called to higher circles in January 1988, he was born in 1914 and the funeral service was held at 12 noon on Friday 9th January 1988 at the Holy Trinity Church Cowes, Isle of Wight. During my happy day spent at the R.S.Y.C. on the 16th July 1989 we were greeted by gentleman commodore Mr. Grinyer where we also enjoyed the warm and friendly company of gentleman the late Mr. Frank Murdock who had sailed on board Endeavour in 1934, and Endeavour II for the challenge in 1937 serving for Hawker Siddley, and sailing as winch and rigging designer and stress and strain expert. Mr. Murdock told me his age with a broad smile and said 'Young man I am 88 years young and after all these years it is just fantastic to hear you talk of our forgotten mariners bringing back treasured memories'. Sadly we never had a reunion before Endeavour left Southampton for a new life in America. After a visit on board we all wished Captain Jon Barrett U.S.A. sailing master of Endeavour and his crew God's blessing and a safe passage. My late friend Mr. Cyril Coates of Tollesbury, focsle cook on board Endeavour, kept the crew happy at all times with hot food, he was called to higher circles on the 17th July 1998 and he and is charming wife, the late Ruby, were extremely kind friends during my many Tollesbury visits to their warm and most friendly home. Cyril lost a brother at sea during the 2nd World War, Sub Lieutenant Coates. My friend Mr. Reg Broome, a retired business gentleman, served and sailed at sea during the 2nd World War with Mr Cyril Coates R.N. and

A much treasured photograph of the Author taken with loyal friends of Tollesbury, the late Mr. and Mrs. Ruby and Cyril Coates.

Cyril was a master baker serving on board as focsle cook and he managed under very difficult circumstances to provide the gallant crew members on board with hot soup during the typhoon working only on a primus stove.

Mr. Coates was called to higher circles at his home in Tollesbury on the 17th July 1998 aged 86 years.

Mr. Jim Chainey of Tollesbury on war service. The late Frank Bloome of Walton on the Naze, a brother of Reg, was Coxswain of the Walton lifeboat for many years and along with his loyal and gallant crewmembers was responsible for saving many lives at sea. In 1936 the late Charles Hipkin, a serving crew member, was so dedicated and keen to perform his duty he dived fully clothed off the end of the pier at Walton and swam and caught the lifeboat up to help save his fellowmen. Back to Endeavour II for a moment, as Captain George Williams was buried at sea 150 miles west of the Azores, it was a known fact when Danny Nichols the good second cook from Scotland stood alone and sang the lovely old ballad 'How near to a tear, to a smile', the hardened crew members broke down and cried gently, including a brilliant hardened sailorman Muller White of Gosport. Endeavour during 1934-37. Crew member the late skipper Jim Cann of Port Isaac, Cornwall ,resided Hythe Side of Southampton and along with his charming wife Blanche, who sailed with him for many seasons to the Mediterranean on board the Motor Yacht Sylvia. Jim had also skippered the fabulous sailing yacht Cynara. He served at sea R.N. during the 2nd World War on mine sweepers, being a highly respected sailorman and rigger. A man I had known for many years and exchanged regular Christmas cards with from 1947 until God's calling. He died at an Esso dinner and dance aged 78 Christmas 1985 at Fawley, Southampton. The good boatswain serving on board Endeavour was the late William Granville Mutton (known as Dan) of Port Isaac, Cornwall, (another grand shipmate and loyal friend). Dan and I first palled up yachting after the 2nd World War when we were serving two yachts owned by the late shipping line director, a most kind gentleman to our crew members, both cruising and ashore, Mr. Jack Bilmar of the Stanhope Shipping Company. Dearest Dan, a most trustworthy friend, sent to me his last Christmas card in December 1995 and said in scribble 'Sorry Jeff, I cannot write much, what else do you b--- well expect! I am 95 years old!' That card is still much treasured. Sadly Dan was called to higher circles on the 25th November 1995 but he had made sure to send my card, he is gone but not forgotten. He was a free style Cornish wrestler. I much enjoyed my time at sea and ashore with many Cornish ship mates and in 2002 received many Christmas cards from my Port Isaac grand shipmates, the late Fred and Frankie Grills. It was also an honour to know personally the late Captain McKillop from Scotland who was the master of the brand new M.Y. Phillante which carried 80 private crewmembers. As a lad I saw her in the building process with her bow overhanging the pavement down Lower William Street, Northam. Special permission was obtained from the city council. Northam was my Mother's, native home, and having 17 brothers and sisters, together with 58 Northam cousins on my Mother's side of the family, we would often take my grandfather's wheelbarrow down to

All ship shape and ready to leave Southampton sailing for America on the 16th July 1989.

This photograph portrays the Author leaving from on board Endeavour upon his 60th Birthday, 15th July 1989, after wishing Captain John Barrett, sailing master, God speed and safe voyage; along with his crew members, and sadly, another part of our maritime heritage left dear old England.

Thorneycrofts or Camper & Nicholsons yards for off-cuts of timber. My many good, kind and loveable uncles were either at sea or working as stevedores in the docks; a pattern in life like many a man in Southampton. Sadly, in April 1912, 140 of my mother's school pals had lost a relative overnight on R.M.S. Titanic, a father in most cases. I do have many old photographs, with captions relating to R.M.S. Titanic victims, but that is another story awaiting help for publication.

So let us return to Endeavour and the late Dan Mutton. Dan served as boatswain on board Shamrock V in 1930 for the 5th attempt to regain the America's Cup under the command of the late Captain Ned Heard with 1st mate Jack Gempton of Brixham. Sir Thomas Lipton tried in vain to regain the cup and in doing so provided much employment for hundreds of men with the saying "If it will make a better boat, shovel on the pound notes", but it was not to be. My great uncle the world famous captain Robert Wringe commanded Shamrocks I, II and III over the many yachting seasons. He sadly died at his home, Sandy Hook, in Ladysmith Avenue, Brightlingsea, aged 64 years, on the 24th February 1924. Captain Robert was married to my grandfather's sister Emma Jefferies. I still have a loveable auntie in Southampton aged 84 years, Mrs. Ethel Harfield, whose maritime father was a very popular sailing master in his own right, being the late Jack Diaper from the river Itchen and he served on board Shamrocks in 1901 and 1902 as 2nd mate. So now back to Endeavour and boatswain Dan Mutton. Dan as also a good radio operator and tried so desperately hard to keep the waterlogged transmitter in communication with the outside world and shipping. Dan spent his life caring for his dearest mother whom he truly worshiped. He managed to despatch from Endeavour, in mid channel, to a Daily Mail correspondent a letter to his mother which was delivered to the silver haired widowed mother aged 75 years. She was overjoyed when the correspondent handed the letter over at Falmouth. The letter read as follows:- "Dearest Mother, The crew keeps telling me there is plenty of mutton on board if we should run short of food. It is Sunday, the Sabbeth, today and we are 500 miles from land so with a nice breeze we should be there in 3 days. God has been kind to us. We had a bad night when we were lost from M.Y. Viva but have had it fairly good since. Well dear, the first English news we got by radio was that we were lost, but we were sailing home under our own sail. Captain Heard aske,d me if I could send out a message by wireless so I sent it out about a dozen times that night. The message was picked up, but we were flooded out by seawater, causing the yacht great damage. The next night we all listened to the news again. There was no mention of us but the following night we heard that someone had picked up our message so we all felt easier as we knew you would have heard the same by radio. We also heard the sad news of the death of Captain George Williams of Endeavour II, we were surprised as he was quite well when we left. Well, my dear mother, I will write a little each day until we sail into Gosport so I will close now." The letters continued. Dan, a most kind man, would often come into my Northam, Southampton grandmother's home in Lower York Street, my grandmother who was the well known and

Camper & Nicholsons Gosport, famous yacht designers and builders.

On left of photograph, gentleman Mr. Arthur Nicholson holding nautical conversation with the world famous Captain Ned Heard of Tollesbury, home village of many a good fisherman and yachtsman.

A fantastic live shot photograph racing at Rhode Island U.S.A. Part crew on for'd starboard bow. Captain Ned Heard and also his right hand man, 1st mate the late Jack Gempton of Brixham. Also my late friend boatswain the late Dan Mutton of Port Isaac, Cornwall; he had nerves of steel.

Famous Endeavour 1937 crew members all named nationwide within the JJ collection.
Owner:- Mr. Andreae - London Banker, kind gentleman yacht owner.

Crew members for'd to aft.
(1) Robert Parker, river Itchen Mastheadsman No.2 at age 18 the youngest serving crew member.
(2) Jim Stubbins
(3) Bill Lewis
(4) Horace Chatterton
(5) Ted Heard Jnr. Aged over 90 years
(6) Cyril Coates, late focsle cook
(7) Late Slim Pengelly, Looe, Cornwall, killed Gosport High Street 1937 on motorcycle
(8) Late Harry Jumbo Randall, Hythe, Southampton, known to author JJ
(9) Late Dann Mutton, Port Isaac, boatswain, friend and shipmate of author JJ
(10) Late Neville Gurton A1 sailorman
(11) Captain John Abrams, brilliant navigator who along with Captain Ned Heard brought Endeavour and crew safely home to England.

Endeavour had sailed almost 3,000 miles across the Atlantic. After her tow rope had parted with M.Y. Viva II commanded by Captain Grant Endeavour broke loose 170 miles East of New York. She had been missing for 13 whole days and was first sighted by the 3rd officer on board the British Tanker SS Cheyenne off Ireland. The Tanker was mastered by Captain Alcock of Newcastle. After 16 hard days passage Endeavour sailed into Gosport on October 1st 1937. He was still fondly remembered by the surviving members of the Endeavour crew for all his efforts.

Eight of Endeavour crew members do not appear within this photograph.

respected Mrs. Harfield. She lived around the homes of many R.M.S. Titanic victims. Two Mrs. Longs resided next door to my grandparents. The two brothers (husbands of these ladies), Will and Arthur, both perished on that bitter cold night on April 15th 1912 when 1700 poor souls perished on board Titanic, and prior to the 2nd World War I would visit the homes of the two Mrs. Longs and other widows and families. God bless all their memories. No one can take away this gift that was given to me in my life.

Back to Endeavour. The yacht Alert in 1937 first sighted Endeavour as she had passed the Lizard through the dangerous Manicle rock. Janer Snell, coxswain of the Falmouth lifeboat with his sharp eagle eyes first sighted Endeavour. Janer had served and sailed on board the J class yachts and had also crewed on board Shamrock V under the command of captain Ned Heard. Not forgetting in my story my shore going pals from Port Isaac, Cornwall who had also served on board Shamrock V in 1932 when the

West Country crew members had their own choir on board and were heard on the radio programme 'In Town Tonight'. God bless your memories. Janer Snell had also served on board the big Astra owned by Mr. Paul of the Ipswich Mills. The yacht Alert approached Endeavour, and at Janer's first sighting of the yacht she looked magnificent as she was sailing under mizzen trysail, foresail and jib. She forged along as gracefully as a swan. The sight of her slender lines, her long blue hull, her towering mast and sails together with the bronzed crew. Eight of these were remarkable sailor men from Tollesbury. The crew were all more interested in the little ship approaching than in the aeroplanes which roared their welcome overhead, but they gripped their hearts and won the admiration of them all. Janer Snell hailed his friend Captain Heard, simple were their words but warm their welcome. 'You've had a nice blow' said Janer. 'Glad to see you Janer', said Captain Heard. These writings are true, most sincere and honest; written from a standpoint as never written before, with so much personal knowledge, connections and intimate details of the forgotten mariners of Great Britain, whom I befriended over the years, and proudly sailed with many.

First to board Endeavour, and he approached Captain Heard with his hand outstretched, was a very young Daily Mail reporter, Mr John Rickan. He was welcomed by the hand of Captain Heard who quietly said to him, 'I am glad to know any friend of Janers, please tell my wife that I, our son Ted and also my courageous crew members, are longing to get home'. I must add within my story that Ted Heard Jnr., 92 years of age (in 1998), a-man who sailed on board Shamrock V America's Cup Challenge in 1930 as the ships carpenter, and also served Endeavour 1937 has been, along with other mariners, a pillar of strength, with both knowledge and material towards the J.J. collection and I pray that all their memories live on. The owner of Endeavour was a most caring and kind man, Mr. Andreae. The yacht arrived in Gosport on the 1st October 1937 and a bequest was made by the late gentleman, Sir Thomas Sopwith, owner of Endeavour II and also of the brand new motor yacht M.Y. Phillant,e that Mrs. Paul would take the Endeavour's wheel and steer her into Gosport to a heroes welcome for both yacht and crew. M.Y. Phillantie, which was over 1,000 tons and carried 80 private crew members, played a very important role during the misadventures under the command of the late captain McKillop not forgetting the two late Frost brothers of Tollesbury, Jack and Frank, who served on board M.Y. Phillantie as chief and 2nd stewards, all their friends, relatives and loved ones and for all their friends and relatives on shore who were caused so much grave concern. Gentleman Sir Thomas Sopwith who was indeed a great aviator pioneer, inventor and sportsman. Endeavour sailed into Gosport on the 1st October 1937 to a heroes welcome with Endeavour under snow white sails and sunlight. Both yacht owners, Sir Thomas Sopwith and Mr. Andreae, showed overwhelming kindness to these gallant sailormen, and greeted all their Tollesbury relatives with warmth and friendship, the latter being the best ship of all. Sir Thomas Sopwith allowed his brand new luxury yacht M.Y. Phillante to be used as a luxury hotel for which the good maritime families of Tollesbury still praise him 65 years on. He was called to higher circles on January

F. Frost (Tollesbury).
chief steward on board M.Y. Phillante 919370.

27th 1989 aged 101 years. As stated within my recordings, which are sacred to all their memories, plus a lifetimes further research and work spent knowing the masters and mariners of Great Britain with not one door being closed in my face during my research, which has been carried out entirely at my own expense and for which, I fear, I have received so little recognition. However, most sadly many professional people with the power to save and publicise our heritage, which is a most sacred possession, have done very little to recognise my lifetimes maritime works.

As one journeys through life it is great to recall happy times of bygone days sparing a thought for all our forsaken mariners, and this short story will prove the point. Many came into my life, including yachtsmen, whilst serving as mate with the late respected, well liked gentleman captain Thomas Watts of Padstow, who later made his home in Southampton. He spent many years as yacht master Mediterranean cruising. Not forgetting also a well liked friend captain Donald Shaw from the Outer Hebrides, he too made his home in Southampton. He served as first mate on board many yachts sailing with captain Watts, including the fabulous M.Y. Fair Lady. Captain Donald Shaw was a great friend of many a good fisherman and yachtsman from the Outer Hebrides and Scotland, and for many years, still serving on board Mr. Harry Hyam's magnificent M.Y. Shemara. Not forgetting as well a good friend for many years, gentleman Mr Larrie Valla who is still serving as the chief engineer. Endeavour 1934 America's Cup challenge. The Late Captain Thomas Watts, whom I greatly admired as a brilliant seaman and jovial and kind man to cruise with on board M.Y. Giroflee in the early 1960s, cruising mostly the West Country with our kind and respected yacht owner gentleman Mr. Mckay, a wealthy man who during the 1926 depression had built the fabulous 200 ton Elke, which was mastered by a sail master who was the father of captain Thomas Watts, and on board M.Y. Giroflee our good engineer, and most likeable shipmate and 'going ashore pal' was Dick Farrow of St. Ives, Cornwall. I had also sailed with Dick's cousin John 'Lofty' Farrow. Dick's uncle had survived the St. Ives lifeboat tragedy and was known in St. Ives as Survivor. On Endeavour 1934 captain Watts was indeed the sailorman who drafted a protest letter on behalf of the crew to Sir Thomas Sopwith requesting £50.00 danger money to cross the fierce and treacherous Atlantic to challenge for the America's Cup. Fourteen crew members resigned over this sad dispute and sailormen the late Reg Tillett and Charlie Hempstead died broken hearted of not taking an active roll under the command of captain G. Williams for the challenge. The crew members were replaced with amateurs. The late Sir Thomas Sopwith was, like myself, a man of strong principals but keeping out of political and religious arguments which are like the Atlantic, too deep for me to argue with. However I must add that knowing the first hand honest facts and as an honest maritime author, maritime historian and retired mariner my own private belief is that Sir Thomas was indeed within his rights and powers to refuse this request, which should have been made prior to signing Board of Trade Agreement to sail, and not after signing. Captain Thomas Watts was indeed a great friend of the late mariner Teddy Coppin, a 1922-23-24 Flying Cloud seaman along with the A1 sailorman boatswain the late Mr Brown of the River Itchen. Flying Cloud was converted into a fabulous yacht for the late Duke of Westminster and involved 500 companies. She was commanded by a captain Underwood and all the facts and old photographs are within the J.J. collection. Teddy Coppin resided in Cannes, South of France and ran, as manager, a ships chandlery business for Hibbs of Brightlingsea, Hibbs who also owned several trading barges. I must add that Captain Watts was indeed a most honest and placid gentleman to sail with and a brilliant conversationalist (myself being an avid listener). Mr. Coppin's son, speaking fluent French and German, was dropped on the first day of the 2nd World War, by parachute, behind enemy lines to report to British Intelligence. Sadly he was captured, tried and shot as a spy on the first day of the war, a bloody war with much heartache for many, including my father in law who was called to rest on the 16th April 1997 aged almost 90 years, and the mention of heartache when one and all should hold true values and respect towards those who did so much and asked so little. The point of this story, founded on facts, is that we had a fabulous Golden Day held in Brightlingsea with aircraft flying over the River Colne at very low altitude, a magnificent sight, but unfortunately very poor weather. The flags were hoisted nicely around the Cinque Port Town with memorabilia displayed in the High Street windows and honour scrolls of our fallen heroes, and rightly so, plus local men who were prisoners of war. This was a very sad day for my wife Jean, as her father's name was not permitted on that scroll, his offence being that he was a month old baby arriving at Brightlingsea from London and not classed as a Brightlingsea man.

My mariner friend late Navie Mussett of Tollesbury, was one of everybody's favourites, God bless his memory. He was a world travelled sailorman and was a prisoner of war in the 1st World War and very ill treated, but was still fishing at the age of 90 years young still with a marvellous sense of humour and his saying 'One is not pulling a rope until ones feet are pulled through the deck'. I much enjoyed visits to his Tollesbury home, and also sailormen Hector Frost and his son John, fondly remembered yachtsmen and fishermen, gone but not forgotten.

This photograph portrays one of Endeavours former crew members saying his last fare ye well, sacred to his memory, Jim Mussett of West Mersea. His comment was "You caused us all a great deal of heartache you proud old lady of the sea."

Jim was on board M.Y. Viva II during the height of the hurricane when Endeavour parted with her tow rope. Viva II was commanded by the late Captain Grant of Southampton.

Mr. Jim Mussett, sailorman and friend was called to higher circles on the 21st July 1997 aged 92 years.

Tragedy befell Navvy Mussett and his extremely kind wife and family during the 2nd World War when their mariner son, Neville Mussett, perished at sea within our local estuary along with captain Gunner Potter and his good son Gordon, when their fishing smack C.K. Express struck a mine. Gordon was also a brilliant man working aloft as mast headsman. He had raced in America, under his fathers command, racing on board the big Astra. Keith Mussett, a good former yacht skipper and I, often linked up for a good yarn during the 50s and 60s down the West Country. Tollesbury maritime - mostly all the good household names of the mariners of this quaint and friendly village along the Essex coast, I have tried to mention. Men who served on board the world famous Shamrocks, and mariners who sailed and raced under the command of the world famous yacht masters, captains Heard, Turner, Sycamore, Steve Barbrook and Robert Wringe, the latter being my great uncle. Sailormen Will Riley, Ted Heard, Tom Sampson, Theodore Lewis, sadly drowned from the 23 metre Shamrock 2nd April 1924. Sailorman Tom Sampson had served on board Shamrock III in 1903 racing off Hunters Quay on the Clyde when caught in a squall of wind and losing the 160 foot mast and causing the loss of one life, that of Mr. Collier of Wivenhoe.

My first real taste of yachting after the 2nd World War was indeed serving and sailing with the late skipper Percy Howe of Tollesbury on board the magnificent yawl yacht Wayward III, owned by the late gentleman Mr. Jameson a company director of Shell Oil. Mr Howe, had sailed with captain George Williams as a serving crew member on board Endeavour for the America's cup challenge in 1934, and had also served on board Endeavour II in 1937. Both the late Mr. and Mrs. Howe, Percy and Agnes, showed myself much kindness. They left their native homeland to fulfil a lifetime ambition and made their home in one of my favourite places, Lymington in Hampshire. Mr. Howe loved sailing and had also served for many racing seasons on board the 12 metre Flika prior to the 2nd World War. These boats were fast but wet boats on which my late uncle, Harold Stroud of Whitstable in Kent, skippered the

A much treasured photograph of the late sailorman and friend, Jim Mussett of West Mersea. Endeavour crew member welcomed home from an horrific ordeal by A1 sailorman Gordon Potter of Tollesbury being a superb workingman aloft, serving the big Astra, racing in America under his fathers command.

The cruel sea was soon to claim three more Tollesbury mariners as sadly Captain Gunner Potter, sailing master, who was the owner of the Tollesbury Smack C.K. Express struck a sea mine during the 2nd World War. He was killed along with his son Gordon plus a loving son of the late mariner Navvy Mussett, Neville.

The late skipper Percy Howe of Tollesbury had served and sailed under the command of Captain George Williams 1934 and 1937, also sailorman Hector Frost.

Mr. Howe after the 2nd World War was indeed my first good yachting skipper on board the fabulous yawl sailing yacht Wayward III owned by gentleman Mr. Jamerson. M.B.E. company director of Shell Oil and a most kind yacht owner; residing at Frinton on Sea.

yacht Blue Merlin a 12 metre class in 1937-38. Uncle Harold was the serving mate on board the 12 metre Lucilla skippered by a great sailorman and fisherman of Burnham on Crouch, the late captain William Deacon, when on August 6th 1930 the gigantic 24 metre racing cruiser Lulworth ran down Lucilla off Cowes, Isle of Wight, sadly trapping and drowning Mr. W. Saunders of Burnham on Crouch who was a serving crew member. Ted Ashby also of Burnham on Crouch, was serving as Captain Deacon had injured his arm and uncle Harold Stroud saved his life. Uncle joined Shamrock, was 2nd mate with captain Ned Heard. It was soon learnt of the retirement of another brilliant sailorman and Solent pilot, Mr. Joe Giles of Cowes, Isle of Wight, who was serving on board the royal racing cutter Britannia as 1st mate. When captain Heard learned of this he said to my uncle 'Go for it Harold, before it is too late'. My uncle served and raced on board Britannia as 1st mate until just prior to the death of His Majesty, King George V, a great sportsman and sailorman who passed away peacefully on Monday 20th January 1936 after a reign of more that 25 glorious years. By his death we lost a beloved leader who through troubled and anxious years shared equally in his peoples joys and sorrows. May His soul rest in peace.

The Homecoming of Endeavour in 1937

A voyage that caught the public fancy

Welcome as for a cup winner

The voyage of Endeavour I, never has a yacht been welcomed home with such blasts from the press trumpets which greeted Endeavour I, sailing up the channel into Gosport, as stated in story "graceful as a swan". One might be pardoned for imagining that at least she has brought home her America's Cup to our shores, instead of having merely acted as a "trial horse" to her sister ship which sadly failed in this project.

I always felt at home with so many mariners, with warmth and kindness by so many and their families, paying many visits for many years (god bless their memory), there was great rejoicing in the village of Tollesbury, when the good news was received that Endeavour I had been located 260 miles South West

A much treasured photograph taken with loyal friends enjoying our get togethers, enjoying nautical conversation. Royal British Legion. Cowes, Isle of Wight.

Left to right: Kenneth Wheeler, Arthur Wheeler who made his home in Shanklin, Isle of Wight 1989 upon retirement. J.J. Author, centre of photograph. Next gentleman Jim, the late Mr. Jim Higgins 2nd World War R.N. Jim and his lady wife, Bonnie served at the Royal Yacht Squadron for 18 years. Jim was head steward and President of the R.B.L. He was sadly called to higher circles in January 1997. On right of photograph, a young at heart 93 year old mariner friend, world travelled as ships carpenter on board many famous yachts, all named in main stories. Jack served his apprenticeship in Aldous shipyard, Brightlingsea when his family members made their home in Tower Street after the 1st World War. Jack's sailing master father, late Captain Tom Felton mastered Sir Walter Preston's MP. steam yacht S.Y. Lorna for 18 years. Jack's brother, Captain Tom Felton jnr. aged 96 when called to rest at his Miami home U.S.A 1990 was master of M.Y. Malarne owned by gentleman Sam Speagles U.S.A., a film producer. Captain Tom Felton was also master of American Passenger Liners. S.S. Bahama Star, 20,000 tons and also Emerald Isles 11,000 tons.

of Fasten Rock off the coast of Ireland, and the crew, seven of whom belonged to Tollesbury, all predicted throughout the ordeal that Captain Ned Heard, with nerves of steel would fetch the yacht and all her crew members safely back to England under her own sail. The good news was received in a message to the vicarage from Lloyds, and was conveyed to the homes of the mariners on the yacht, immediately. The whole village was filmed for the news reels, and all the school children assembled in the playground and where seen to be giving three hearty cheers, with the late Mrs Florence Heard as the central figure, the church bells were rung and recorded, the menfolk were busy drinking the health of fellow mariners, skipper and crew, and the home place of so may popular and well loved Tollesbury yachtsman and fisherman. It was almost named "Hollywood" overnight with films added and taken of Endeavour and Endeavour II on arrival into Gosport to a hero's welcome and Civic Reception. Captain Edward Carrington Heard was called to higher circles on November 30th 1947 aged 68 years; his lady wife Florence was reunited with her husband and died on December 24th 1960 aged 84 years. I must add in my story it was reported Endeavour I was sighted of the Azores and reported by Captain Alcock (Brilliant Master) of the British Tanker Cheyenne. This fine gentleman had known how ruthless and how kind, the sea can be, having lost two brothers at sea.

J.J. Collection by kind permission of Gentleman Mr. Keith Beken and his son Kenneth of Beken of Cowes, Isle of Wight. (c)

Mr. Beken and family are world renowned marine photographers and a pleasure to know and respect. Mr. Keith Beken F.R.P.J. marine photographer to H.R.H. The Duke of Edinburgh.

Photograph taken July 1994 left to right:

J. Jefferies, Jack Felton, Mariner Supreme aged 94 years, world travelled yachtsman being a son of a very popular yacht master the late Captain Tom Felton of Southampton who mastered after the 1st World War Sir Walton Preston M.P.'s fabulous steam yacht Lorna for 18 years. The yacht was always laid up during the winter months in Brightlingsea, in Aldous shipyard. The 1st mate was a Mr. Reiss of Falmouth.

So I will end my little story by saying here is a prayer "For all they that go down to the sea in ships, and do their business in great waters". These see the works of The Lord, and his wonders in the deep (Psalm 107 23/24). And under every sun are the nameless burial mounds for sailors whose ships went down because there are none to do them homage, none to relate their annals, none to exalt their virtues. This my good readers is my prayer for all who go down to the sea in ships. God bless their memory and God bless you one and all for reading my recordings.

JJ

McCaws Groceries and Provisions where the hearty crew members catered for all their needs and requirements, with mutual respects and friendship.

Below:
A 1937 drawing by an unknown Tollesbury school child.

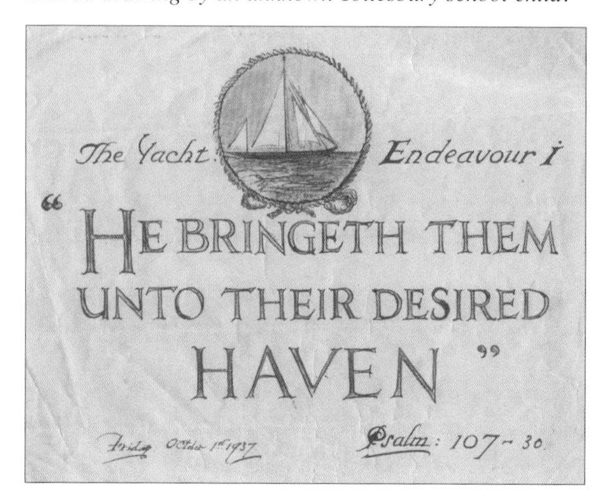

Ranger Master and Crew. Hand picked crew all first class sailors. Captain G. Monsell.

Shamrock V 1930

The last of Sir Thomas Lipton's American Cup Challengers. He was, the worlds best ever, loser and sportsman, and he died soon after this challenge at over 80 years of age. He was made a member of the Royal Yacht Squadron, just prior to God's calling. Sir Thomas, was a great sportsman and a great benefactor to the poor folk of Glasgow, and he was greatly respected by his officers and crewmembers from all parts of England. I myself, feel extra proud of the fact that my great uncle, the famous captain Robert Wringe mastered over the yachting season and American Cup Challengers, such famous yachts as Ailsa Bona and Shamrocks I, II & III. During my youth, and also during my own yachting career, it was a joy and honour, to know four of the brilliant shipwrights, who helped to build Shamrock V in 1930. Built by the famous Camper & Nicholsons. These four tradesmen, grew up and worked amongst many of the Northam families, who in April 1912 had lost so many loved ones on board RMS Titanic, White Star Shipping Company.

Photograph, taken middle of 1950's in Camper & Nicholsons yacht yard, men as follows:

Bert Fox, Jimmy Medway, Bill Long & Fred Moore. In 1980 when Shamrock V was rebuilt these brilliant shipwrights were still working on this great yachts restoration, a creation all by the human hand.

October 9, 1937—WEEKLY ILLUSTRATED

HOW ENDEAVOUR CAME HOME

SIRENS from hundreds of vessels screamed a deafening welcome as *Endeavour I*—missing for a fortnight after her tow-rope parted in a storm off the American coast—glided into Gosport.

For the last miles of her journey up-Channel she had been surrounded by hooting tugs and motor-launches, 'planes carrying press-men and photographers had zoomed above her masts.

Captain Heard and his men were somewhat bewildered by their reception. "Sure, we had a bit of a blow, but on the whole a calm passage," was Capt. Heard's description of an historic voyage—now ended in the happiest way possible.

Safe home at last—Captain Heard and his wife enjoy a joke with the Mayor of Gosport.

The log books were lost overboard, and a pencilled record was kept on a hatchway.

The first mate, John Gempton (centre), gets his last orders from the captain.

Broad, beaming smile belongs to Jim Stubbins, holding David, one of twins.

Dan Mutton—got tired of his name. They all said they'd kill and eat him if food ran short.

Joe Huglow, the cook, said: "We were just a ship of steel, under water most of the time. I had an easy job."

Robert Parker was at the wheel at the height of the storm when the tow-rope parted.

Harry German, caught by camera, giving his wife a kiss.

Ringing a welcome from the famous firm of Ratsey's, who made Endeavour's sails.

And this is Capt. Abrahams, the navigator—who had a big hand in getting the boat safely home.

A bright moment when the beer comes aboard. The crew never knew they had so many friends.

Another re-united family—C. Randall with his wife and daughter Doreen.

7

Page from, Weekly Illustrated, October 9th 1937

An Editorial from The New York Times of Wednesday, September 29, 1937

ENDEAVOUR WAS A LADY

LIKE KIPLING'S LINER, *Endeavour I* was a lady. Like other cup defenders and challengers, she was built to win races in coastal waters, under moderate winds, and not to take it on the nose, all alone, in the wilderness of the western ocean. When she made transatlantic voyages it was intended that she should be towed by a polite and gentlemanly escort with the aid of steam or gasoline. One would as soon have set a race horse to hauling sand as to expose *Endeavour I* to what deep-water seamen consider real weather. Consequently her accidental abandonment in mid-ocean seemed, as the days went by without news, to be the end of the story for vessel and crew.

Just what happened has not been related in detail at this writing. We do not know just how Captain Ned Heard and his sailors managed to keep her right side up and pointed toward Gosport, England, which was the place where they wanted to go. A racing yacht strikes a landlubber as a perilous conveyance when the wind gets to a point where an old-fashioned square-rigger captain would begin to scratch his head and wonder whether or not it was worth while to take a reef in the topsails. *Endeavour I* must have stood on her ear and sat on her west end all the way over.

Captain Ned Heard is probably going to hear his strenuous voyage referred to more times than he can count as a saga, and in the end he will get tired of that word. Let us say, then, that it was not a saga. It may not even have been especially heroic, for, after all, Captain Heard and his men wanted to go on living, and the surest way to do that was to bring their ship to port. But the trip will have to be described as a feat of seamanship that no sailors of any age could have excelled. Cool, calm skill and resolute endurance must have stood at the helm, trimmed the sails and somehow climbed the reeling deck. One tries to picture it, but fails, and perhaps picks up Conrad's "Typhoon" or "The Nigger of the Narcissus," in order to come at truth by way of fiction,

A SHORT STORY

S.Y. SAPPHIRE II, owners Lord and Lady Fairhaven (American Oil Tycoons), great benefactors to Great Britain during the 2nd World War.

The luxury yacht, laid up and fitted out each session, in Camper and Nicholson's fine yacht yard, Southampton.

Following in my maritime father's footsteps and being the 6th generation on my father's side of the local Jefferies and Brasted families to be Freeman of the River Colne of Royal Charter Birthright, my forebears held upon the tidal grounds in the north and south channel around Underwood's Hard. Also Royal Charter Ground Rights Freehold, as previously mentioned within my works, together with 1,000 years leasehold ground rights. Many tidal plots were recorded as Jefferies/Aldous, Aldous/Jefferies, Peggs/Jefferies. The late George Peggs had been shipmate with my father prior to the 1st World War serving with members of the Vanderbilt families, and his son, George 'Knocker' Peggs was also a shipmate in 1937 with father on board Sunbeam II owned by Lord Runciman of the shipping line. His Lordship held his own master mariners qualifications. The yacht was under the command of and A1 sailing master, Captain Nicholas, a Danish sailorman. Sunbeam raced around the islands in Canada with the tall ships. Dad, like myself, always got along very well with our jovial Cornish shipmates on board Sunbeam II. On board were serving sailors from Brightlingsea, the late AB Charles Branch, RN 2nd World War, and a retired Customs Officer. Late George Martin, and the late Charles Hempstead who was in 1934 Endeavour AB. He was a man who, sadly, did not sail being one of the crew members who resigned over the pay dispute. Many Sunbeam II mariners from Appledore, West Coast, had been jovial shipmates of my father, many grand sailormen from St. Ives and Port Isaac, Cornwall. Big Ginger Harry May was boatswain on board the 24 metre Lulworth for 11 years under the command in 1926 of a famous sailing master of the river Itchen, Captain Charles Bevas. The 1st mate was the late Captain Archie Hogarth, Clydeside. The 2nd mate was also a brilliant man of sail, the late Mr. George Frances, local. This mariner I myself was apprenticed to in the river Colne. Bert Piper was also a jovial shipmate from Brixham, Devon serving in 1926 on board Lulworth. In 1936 Tom 'Chaddie' Chadburn was also a serving seaman on board Sunbeam II and he was one the most jovial friends any man could wish to be shipmates with, myself included.

And it pleases J. J. to know that the famous 24 metre Lulworth is nicely rebuilt for her proud gentlemen owner.

When Chaddie sailed on board with us on MY Virginia RYS as foc'sle cook, he was followed by Dick Stevens of Port Isaac in the 1950's with grand fellow shipmates from St. Ives, 'Lofty' Farrow and Jimmy Cocken. The late Jimmy had sailed with my father, world cruising, on board SY Sapphire II, RYS during the 1930's. The yacht had 58 private crewmembers. Also a shipmate of father, from Port Isaac, was Dan Mutton who was called to rest 25th December 1995 aged 95 years. Dan and I were shipmates after the 2nd World War along with sailorman and friend Freddie Grills from Port Isaac. We crewed together on board Mr. Jack Bilman's two yachts after the 2nd World War. Dan was boatswain on board Shamrock V in 1930 and boatswain of Endeavour in 1937.

In 1931 Dan was still a serving boatswain on Shamrock V with good Tollesbury hardy mariners many of whom skippered their own smacks during the winter months, stowboating until the yachting seasons came round. The elder mariners of Tollesbury, whom many were indeed a joy to know worked the fishing smacks come spring shrimping and landed their catch in Brightlingsea. Most of these were sent to London by train, when we once had railway. Plus 15 local girls pre-war summer time working in field gates. Dock and shrimp picking to be sent to London hotels.

Captain Ned Heard, man of sail with nerves of steel, mastered Shamrock V and it was a most sad day for us all in 1947 when he was involved with the giant ships, that were lying up in the river Blackwater, when this gallant man sadly died on board one of these ships. The brilliant 1st and 2nd mates with Captain Heard on board Shamrock V were Jack Gempton of Brixham and my late uncle, Harold Stoud. He joined the Royal Racing Cutter Britannia as 1st mate 1931 and 1936. My uncle Harold was also the mate on board the 12 metre Lucilla when on August 4th 1931, mastered by captain William Deacon of Burnham on Crouch, it was run down by the 24 metre Lulworth.

My own shore-going pals of Port Isaac, plus some shipmates, when we had good sing songs ashore whilst fitting out and laying up periods were Jack Spry and his brother Bill, Jack Spry landlord of the Golden Lion, Fred and Frank Grills, Gaggy Hoskins, Little Morley, Dick Stevens, Tinker Brown, Jimmy Peters, John Tamsett and many more good songsters. My good pals Norman and Charlie Short, brothers of Port Isaac had served on board Shamrock V in 1931 with Dan Mutton still boatswain, together with many other West Country crew members. They were all brilliant songsters. They appeared on BBC's In Town Tonight. Port Isaac skipper Jim Cann and I were friends for many years. He was an Endeavour sailorman in 1937 and served RNVR on board mine sweepers during the 2nd World War. Jim had skippered MY Sylvia for several years Mediterranean cruising. He also skippered the fabulous ketch yacht Cynara for her owner, the Marquis of Northampton, being a kind gentleman yacht owner, very tall with a military appearance. Jim sent to me a last Christmas card prior to God's calling, the same as dear Dan. Jim died near Christmas 1985 at an Esso dinner and dance, aged 77 years, one evening, close to his home. His lady wife, Blanche, who had also crewed and sailed with Jim each year to the Mediterranean, was with him.

Captain Pat Billings of Port Isaac, home Warsash, Southampton was also a friend and one of my father's grand shipmates, he was also serving on board SY Sapphire II, owned by Lord and Lady Fairhaven USA in the 1930's. Captain Pat Billings was a Cornish Free-Style Wrestler the same us Dan Mutton and big Andrew Steer. Captain Billings mastered MY Cardigrae Vi for many years for the kind yacht owner who was a highly respected gentry folk, Sir Dutton Foreshore, his lady wife and members of their family. He had also served as a seaman on board SY Sapphire II along with my father's shipmates and shore-going pals, Tommy Jewel, Bobby Jewel, Tom Kemp, Ike Jewell from Appledore, Johnny Bull, Gosport. During our runs ashore in Southampton, between the fitting out and laying up periods, my fellow yachtsmen, pals of Port Isaac are as follows: - Fred Honey, Tinker Brown, Dick Stevens, Little Morley, Tom 'Chaddie' Chadburn, Jack Richards, Fred and Frank Grills, Gaggy Hoskins, Jack Spry, his brother Bill Spry, Mark Townsend, Charlie and Norman Short along with 'Brickie' Ernest Holman who was our good owners launchman on board MY Virginia. Brickie had also sailed along with my father on board Sunbeam II in 1937. I must add Gaggy, being Gaggy, whilst we cruised for a six month charter up inside the Arctic Circle with the Duke and Duchess of Westminster, upset her Ladyship and was discharged and paid off in Southampton just prior to Cowes Week in 1951. Up at Bossekop, well inside the Artic Circle, land of the midnight sun. There was no way of returning him home to England. Consequently he had to stay until we returned. The same night, my friend and shipmate, Freddie Grills, had fallen overboard off the boat boom, but that is another story.

Frank Grills, Fred's late brother, a crewmember, would joke about this in my regular Christmas cards about our funny run ashore in 1947. Cruising down the Bay of Biscay on board MY Aronia, mastered by Captain Tim Webster of North Shields, our kind owner was Jack Bilmar, director, Stanhope Shipping Company Northam, Southampton. Our runs ashore we would all pay a banker, being Fred Grills most of the time, £1.00 per man and in those days on our runs ashore on a Friday night, was almost sufficient for all our evening drinks. Late Sam Thomas of Port Isaac would join us also. He had resided in Happy Northam and he had served for 15 years as sailor on board SY Sapphire II, also Bernard Baker, Port Isaac who had sailed with my father. Bernard and I linked

Cardigrae VI. W. Pascoe - Billing Master, R. Dutton Foreshaw - Owner, Mrs Foreshaw - wife, Mrs Foreshaw - Daughter.

up last in Paris in 1955, and met up in Port Isaac 2003, and thank God still in touch in 2005 - skipper Bernard now 87 years young.

MY Virginia RYS was mastered by a brilliant navigator the late Captain Behenna of St. Ives Cornwall, home Southampton. The 1st mate was Mr. Frank Atterton. 2nd mate Edward Pitt DSM who had served on board SY Sapphire for 15 years as boatswain's mate under the boatswain, the late Big Alf Cranfield of Rowhedge, whom was a Valkyrie and Shamrock Sailorman. The late Mr. Pitt our superb boatswain 2nd mate on board MY Virginia always said to me "roll on quarter past four Jeff" steaming in through the Needles Isle of Wight and whilst heading for the fabulous Solent River and our mooring buoy off the Hythe when homeward bound, meaning 415 Burgess Road, Swaything, Southampton. Mr Pitt was proud of his native home of Wivenhoe in Essex. His younger brothers were killed in battle, John and Arthur, during the 1st World War. Mr. Pitt made his home and family in Southampton pre 2nd World War and being RNR served at sea during the 2nd World War, being awarded the DSM for bravery at sea. Mostly all these mariners knew and respectfully called my grandmother Mrs. Florence Harfield, 'Gran'.

Northam, being devastated in April 1912 with the tragedy of RMS Titanic when 140 of my mothers school friends had lost a relative overnight. A father in most cases. With one sailorman Mr Siebert of Brightlingsea and a Mr. Couch from Port Isaac perished who were serving crewmembers.

Back to sailorman Mr. George Peggs and family. Being Nelson Street kind neighbours. Mr. George Peggs Snr. fished for oysters and scallops off the treacherous coast of Holland. After the 1st World War he sailed with hardy fishermen of Stranrar, Scotland. He married a kind lady from Stranrar after

S.Y. SAPPHIRE II. The owners were Lord and Lady Fairhaven, N.Y.Y.C. U.S.A. they were wealthy oil tycoons and great benefactors to Great Britain during the 2nd World war. SAPPHIRE II was mastered by Captain Reveley of Southampton. The First Officer was Mr. Stan Gilbert of Brightlingsea.

making their home and family in Brightlingsea. George Peggs Jnr., known by all as 'Knocker', was indeed a very close friend and shipmate of Tom 'Chaddie' Chadburn of Port Isaac. The last contact I had myself with Chaddie was when he served on board the liner Queen Mary as a vegetable cook. During the 2nd World War George Peggs stayed on board the fabulous 600 ton schooner Creole as RNR, and the yacht was built in teak in Camper & Nicholson's in 1927 and launched as Vira. She was based in Scotland for the purpose of degousing ships during the 2nd World War. A brother of George, Jim Peggs, a friend from my Aldous shipyard days started his shipwright apprenticeship in Aldous in 1940 and in 1946 he joined the Royal Navy as a PO Chippy. I myself was not quite old enough to start in the Aldous shipyard. In 1940 the local creeks in the Colne estuary were frozen solid with ice, upon low water there were just solid blocks of ice. So my friends, Peter Revett, David Gant, the late Harry Moss and Sylvia Stacy who was the daughter of a very kind friend from London family living local at

This fine luxury yacht carried four officers holding Master Mariner's qualifications. Mr Stan Leggerton Chief Engineer (Dovercourt), Mr. Barnard Second Engineer (Rowhedge / Southampton), "Darky" Frank Hedgethorn Fourth Engineer (Wivenhoe). "Big Dutchy" Alf Cranfield , Boatswain for 15 years (Rowhedge), Edward Pitt DSM Boatswain's Mate for 15 years (Wivenhoe / Southampton).

My maritime farther Arthur Jefferies, served several seasons on board Sapphire II, along with his yachtsman friends - Reg Howe (Brightlingsea), Percy Cranfield (Rowhedge), Dan Mutton, Bernard Baker and Sam Thomas (all of Port Isacc).

the start of the 2nd World War, we decided to go down the Hard, our playground, and we walked across to the Stone, 2 fathoms deep at low water. On arrival home mother being mother, with her Northam sense of humour said to me "Where have you been?"

"Walked across the Stone mother."

"Silly bugger, and don't be bloody cheeky. Only Jesus could walk across the water."

"Yes mother" I replied "but when we walked across the top of the creek the water was underneath!"

So my lifetime's recordings, I pray to God, our creator, that all my recordings are beneficial to the good folk of Cornwall. With my favourite song of evening ashore with my Cornish shipmates being "When its lamp lighting time in the valley, in my dreams I'll go back home" with friend Frank Grills with his fabulous piano accordion. Also Brickie Olman, and his favourite song was "These old lavender trousers, John, John, John put your trousers on." All these are treasured memories.

Captain Bundy an A1 sailorman of Southampton mastered the fabulous schooner Creole in 1928. The crew were mostly good West Country sailormen and the ships brilliant carpenter was one of my closest friends. Sailorman Jack Felton of Southampton aged 95 years. He was one of the sons of Captain Tom Felton Snr. who mastered Sir William Preston MP MY Lorna RYS for 17 years in peace after the 1st World War. The brilliant 1st Mate was a Mr. Reiss of Falmouth. Jack was also ships carpenter on board MY Shemara for 17 years in peace and World War 2. Shemara was the 1st ship to attend the dead and wounded from on board the 11,000 ton British tanker SS British Inventor. This ship having safe passage from as far as out East, unescorted and then sadly striking 2 sea mines at the Eastern approach of Weymouth harbour. All the old photographs are within the JJ collection.

Schooner Vira 600 tons, better known as Creole, was built in 1927 by Camper & Nicholson, Northam yard. She was designed by Gentleman Mr. Charles Nicholson for Mr. Cochran of the USA. Captain Albert Death of Brightlingsea first mastered her with most all-local crewmembers. They are indeed named within the JJ collection. Late gentleman Major Pope owned schooner Creole and she was commanded under an A1 sailorman of Southampton the late Captain Bundy. 'Sandy' Phil Davis from the West Country was boatswain. AB's Rod Thomas and many more good sailormen; Bill 'Nipper' Hempstead (who was a school pal of my father) served on board many years as caterer and on 6th December 1928 married a Portsmouth lady. This lady, like my mother who was Northam born and bred, and they both left their native homes to make their homes and families in Brightlingsea.

It was indeed a most sad day on the Royal Racing cutter Britannia when Ernie Friend of Brixham, 2nd mate, was washed overboard and drowned on Easter Monday 1932. With all the facts and household names of the brilliant sailormen of Looe included within my main story. My friend yachtsman fisherman 'Big Ginger' the late Sam Shears of Brixham took over the 2nd mates position, and my late uncle Harold Stroud was indeed the 1st mate on board Britannia from 1931-36.

It is still JJ's pleasure to visit my lifetime's fisherman friend Mr Derek Leavett: Whom for many years sailed and worked in harmony with his father skipper owner late Mr Bobby Leavett. A mariner whom during the 1920's yachting seasons had served on board the famous RRC Britannia also racing schooner Westward. Derek purchased his own boat C.K Helen and Violet after the Second World War. From the late Mr William Annis of local - who was a yachtsman and fisherman. Dereck at eighty six years of age still enjoys our nautical yarns and have recently reminded me how the three Tollesbury fishing smacks were renamed - 'the Piano fleet' through bribes - and New Road was nicknamed 'Piano Junction' as all three owners resided there. His brothers Peter and Paul Leavett also served many years fishing.

With the late supreme sailor Billy Wilkinson being a friend and adding to my lifetimes recording.

J.A. Jefferies. Retired mariner, author and historian.

relatives in Northam when in 1936 my Uncle Horace Parker was struck in the head by the main sheet block on board sailing barge Lord Kitchener and, sadly, he died the following day at his rented cottage down below Millbank Street, no. 1, Tramway Cottages.

My late Uncle Ali Bell of 111, Millbank Street, Northam in 1938, and serving as a fireman on board liner Empress of Britain, he was due to become an interpreter on board ship but sadly fell a total distance between decks of 90 feet and, landing feet first, he lay in Southampton General Hospital for 2 years. My loveable Uncle Ali was called to higher circles when God finally opened the Golden Gate in 1968.

Yacht owner, Lord William Waldorf Astor, who died in 1966. He was the owner of MY Deianeira in the early 60's. The Late Captain Behenna of St. Ives, Cornwall. Photograph was taken on the bridge of the MY Deianeira in Monte Carlo harbour when Mediterranean cruising with Lord Astor.

The late Captain Behenna was a world travelled yacht master and served during the 2nd World War on board a deep sea Admiralty tug.

John Jacob Astor perished on board RMS Titanic 15th April 1912, where on board the 1st Class passengers represented the cream of Anglo American Society. The wealthiest among them was undoubtedly 42 year old JJ Astor, great grandson of the wealthy fur trader. He extended the family wealth through real estate acquisitions. William Waldorf Astor was held in great esteem by all his serving crewmembers. (All of whom were known to JJ).

Just to mention a few from Southampton, the late Jim Ballard, mate, Edie Nichols, engineer, Freddy Trim, engineer. Point of interest Edie Nichols and Freddy Trim grew up in Northam amongst RMS Titanic victims.

Many of her crew came from Northam and Chapel. Northam was my mother's place of birth where whole streets were plunged into despair and mourning at the Northam run council school at 1d per child per week. Free dinners for the poor children were provided at Mrs. Brown's home down Millbank Street, Northam, and were prepared in her large sized kitchen.

140 children had lost a relative overnight, a father in most cases. With our own maritime tragedies and

My late Uncle and Auntie, Mr and Mrs Gerrard, Sid and Beatrice schooled with RMS Titanic victims and for many years their home was no. 1, Bond Street in Northam, Southampton. Uncle Sid had served on board The Olympic, The Aquitania, The Mauritania and Majestic as a fireman and he had also been a Southampton stevedore following a pattern in life like many fellow stevedores. Down Bond Street was the Salvation Army Working Mens Home, and during my own seafaring career I often, on my way back to the yachts I served, would stop for a yarn with James Crimmins, he was only 65 years old when died at the Salvation Army Home in Northam in 1956.

As previously stated down Bond Street where at one time the happy homes of the kind Northam folk stood. Our family and myself knew them all. All of them had hearts of gold, it was always known as happy Northam.

James Crimmins was a merchant seaman throughout the 2nd World War. He had served on board a troop ship and escaped death more than once when the ship he served on board was torpedoed in the Mediterranean by a German U Boat. This was the end of his days afloat and through health reasons he worked ashore in Southampton. But James never forgot that cold, bitter night of April 15th 1912 when the impossible really happened. James was a 21year-old, serving as a stoker, deep down inside the ship. When striking the iceberg he always said that the men below felt the bump but were ordered to stick to their posts of duty. They did not realise the dangerous situation that lay ahead until ordered to draw in the fires. When the final order was given 'Abandon Ship every man for himself'. James was only dressed in singlet and shorts when reaching the deck amongst so many passengers and crewmembers. He always quietly spoke of helping where he could and was most fortunate to end up in the last of the 16 lifeboats lowered, full of survivors and at approx 3am he sadly saw people falling and jumping into the ice cold sea. With all the screaming, shouting and the noise, then, suddenly, the silence as this mighty liner stood virtually upright for several minutes before taking her final plunge, two and a half miles deep. A point of maritime interest, the Atlantic Sea bed is shelved, and less deep in many places. James, whilst in the lifeboat for over four hours prior to being picked up by the liner Carpathia, being less well dressed than the wealthy passengers Lady, Mrs. J.J Astor kindly ripped her large sized muff in half and wrapped it around James. He would quietly say this saved his life. James, like many more did not receive one-penny compensation.

When James died in 1956 I was a serving crewmember on board MY Blue Rose. RYS, owner Lord St. Oswald MP, North Wolverhampton, an extremely kind yacht owner. Our captain was the late Edward Pitt DSM of Wivenhoe, home Southampton. Being one of the best mariners I have ever sailed with Mr. Pitt was our boatswain on board MY Virginia RYS during the 1950's and the late Captain Behenna of St. Ives, Cornwall, home Southampton was our master on board MY Virginia. Mr. Pitt serving as boatswain, 2nd mate. Mr. Pitt and I would often walk up Bond Street to see my Gran and many relatives.

These are all treasured memories.

JJ. Retired mariner, author and historian.

Motor Yacht Blue Rose, Paris 1955. Crew members, left to right, Yachtsman J.J. Late Bill Barrett, Engineer, River Itchen, Late Captain Edward Pitt, D.S.M. of Wivenhoe, whose home was Southampton, from pre-war days. Late Jumbo Harry Ford of Gosport, mate. Jimmy Jordon, from Barbados; chef who later was valet to gentleman film producer Mr Sam Speagles, USA on board Motor yacht Malarne. Little Lady Queenie the Irish maid had served over thirty years with Lady St. Oswald. Our extreme kind yacht owner, his Lordship, St. Oswald, member of parliment serving the good people of Wolverhampton.

Outside Buckingham Palace 14th March 1944. After presentation of D.S.M. to Edward Robert Pitt.

From left to right,
Margaret Ann Emma Pitt (mother),
Joyce Pitt (daughter),
Edward Robert Pitt,
John Pitt (son),
Nellie Edith Mountford (sister).

Mariner Edward Pitt, Wivenhoe born and bred, making home and family in Southampton many years prior to the 2nd World War. This man was one of the best ever sailorman whom my father and I had ever sailed with.

John S. Blyth, Lt/Col. USAF Ret., standing by his Mk. XI Spitfire in 1944. The picture was taken from an old transparency and the colours have changed somewhat, the Spitfires were originally painted light blue. He flew alone without guns and had two 36 focal length cameras at the rear. The aeroplane had extra fuel where the guns would be in a fighter.

He flew 53 mission along such targets as Berlin, Munich, Czechoslovakia, the Ruhr, buzz bomb sites, airfields etc. Most of the missions were 30,000ft or above. Fifteen missions were in the F-5 (P-38) and 38 in the Spitfire.

In a personal letter to JJ, dated 28 September 1999, following a chance meeting on a local bus, John S. Blyth wrote:

"After I got off the bus, I went to Tolleshunt Knights Church where 21 members of the Blyth family are buried. My family farmed Abbott's Wick and Barn Hall Farms. Also, they leased land at Cressing Temple.

I got so tired from my travels, I came home two days ahead of time.

Again it was a pleasure to meet you.

Sincerely,

John S. Blyth"

TREASURED MEMORIES OF YACHTING AND SEAFARING THROUGH THE AGES

by J. Jefferies

Captain Luther Gould Sen. of Brightlingsea

Many years have sailed by since first meeting and knowing men of the gallant and courageous Royal Life Boat Service and those of Trinity House, mariners to whom many I proudly served and sailed with, serving as seaman on board Trinity House Tenders, Tending Masters and Crew members, changing the watch on board Trinity House Light Vessels. These sailormen dedicating their lives, protecting fellow man from the perils of the sea, in their hours of need and protection from perils of the deep. Cox'n's and Crew members of the R.N.L.I. included. Knowing these men and respecting them for many years for their bravery and gallantry. Clacton, Walton and Harwich men who put to sea, day and night, in all weathers, to save fellow man, and in years gone by, I myself had spent many a happy hour ashore joining their jovial company and enjoying a nautical yarn. Most of the brave sailormen, plus men of the R.N.L.I. I have recorded in my story. A story of which is also their true stories, including I, myself, the same as all their relatives and loved ones. We hold them strongly to our hearts with fondest affection and I pray to God that they can one and all be remembered within my maritime recordings some day.

Captain Richard Woodman, Master Mariner, maritime author included, a gentleman whom I also greatly respected and sailed with whilst serving on board Trinity House Tender SS Vestal. When during a gale in 1970 we had a bit of a to-do whilst marooned on Beachy Head, tending the lighthouse, when a storm arose. Here listed are just a few names of heroic sailormen who helped to protect Masters and Crew members in the perilous shipping lanes from perils of the sea.

Late Master George Halp, aged 89 years, with 32 years to his credit serving with Trinity House. Ten years as master he had served: L.V. Shipwash, L.V. Outer Gabbard, L.V. Seven Stones, for many years he had served as first mate on board Lowestoft sail and steam trawlers prior to joining the Trinity House service. His Master Mariner father perished at sea and he also lost a brother on board ship, lost with all hands, when striking a mine off Herne Bay during the Second World War. A most sad day for L.V. late Master Mr George Halp, as this tragedy of ship Crew members and a brother was within his sight as he stood helpless.

My friends, Alfred and George Testa, spent their lives working for Trinity House, and shipmates Fred Sole, Ron Elliott and Josh Shepherd, not forgetting two very young seaman Peter Brown of Wivenhoe and Richard Collier of Ramsey who were both tragically killed on shore. God bless their memory.

Retired Mr Gordon Thorpe, who having held the rank of Shore Bosun for many years joined the Trinity House service after his army days in the Second World War, Gordon being the last man in the service to hold a title of Shore Bosun. Gordon, I have known and greatly respected for many years, lost a brother on board the Trinity House ship SS Strathern, a 2,000 ton ship, when the ship stuck a mine off Clacton-on Sea. The ship is a mariners grave for half her crew (16 perished and 16 were saved). Fred Thorpe was crushed to death from fallen metal from the explosion of the mine. Fred having a premonition that he was going to lose his young life at sea with many of his good shipmates who also perished with the ship, as he prepared his possessions prior to sailing, rolled up in a handkerchief, which he left with a friend, a small amount of cash to hand to his father in the event of his death. Many of the Thorpe family members served the ships and Light Vessels sailing out of Harwich. Mr Ben Simpson mastered the Cork Light Vessel, his brother Frank Simpson, sadly drowned boarding a light vessel trying to save a fellow man who was knocked overboard by a ship's fender - his body was not recovered.

Masters remembered: Frank Wright, Ernie Pool, Jack Goldsmith, William Bowles, Bobby Jones (Mastered the Barrow Deep L.V. after the Second World War), Master Archie Smith who survived the loss of Trinity House vessel SS Hurgus during the Second World War. Trinity House serving Light Vessel seamen: Ginger Dugar Betts, Ben Ward (a Harwich man who was slashed in the face by a German bayonet during the First World War), Tom Melay, Ipswich, Harry Pridle, Bill Green (kept Half Moon local Inn at Harwich). Some of these men are recorded in my photographs.

Harry Barnes, Skipper, respectfully well-known ashore and afloat as "Barney". I often enjoyed the jovial company of this Grand Mariner and his lady wife in their Dovercourt home. Barney, a retired mariner from the sea, a man who served the Royal Navy during the Second World War, joining the Trinity House service in 1949, retiring in 1988. He mastered the Light Vessel Galloper and Light Vessel Shipwash and Barrow Deep and in 1970 the Painted Green, the wreck of which laid off the Varne Shoal, for 12 months to protect shipping, with Barney doing his duty, working a month on board ship and a month on shore.

There was an in-shore sea rescue boat on board the wreck marker, Trinity House Light Ship and two extra seaman serving from the steam vessel service. These men were trained as Cox'n's to man the rescue boat under Lieutenant Commander Cooper, a gentleman greatly respected by Skipper Barney and Crew. They saved quite a few lives, these incidents taking place during dense fog. The Green Light

Vessel was stationed off the Varne to protect other shipping from colliding when the tragic loss of 3 ships and much loss of human life occurred. These shipping tragedies taking place at different times. SS Texaco Caribbean, 2nd ship SS Brandenburgh, struck a portion of SS Caribbean. The Greek ship SS Niki, carrying iron ore, came to grief and tragedy. The sad loss of these ships were all within a short space of time, a sad sight I shall always remember, being a serving seaman on board Trinity House ships at the time of the tragedies. I lost my maritime father around the same time, when he died on 20th June 1970.

Light Vessels which once protected shipping from tragedies and perils of the sea are quickly disappearing from our coasts now and are being replaced by unmanned Lambie Buoys automation. The ships were manned by men with special temperament and patience and the ways of the Light Vessel Masters and seamen almost no longer exist regards to manning these Light Vessels. During the era of the gallant Lifeboat Cox'n's and Crew members, manning the old type rowing boats, towed to wrecks by steam pinnaces, then came the motor Lifeboats around our coasts.

At Christmas time a great deal of kindness was organised by these gallant life savers, men who put to sea in all weathers to save fellow man, men of the Lifeboat services and the good townsfolk traders of Clacton-on-Sea, Harwich, Walton, Dover, Margate, Ramsgate and Aldeburgh and around the coasts of England, Scotland and Wales. A special delivery of goodwill from organisations was carried out when, on Boxing Day, Lifeboat Cox'n's and Crew members, plus some members of the organisation, put to sea, weather permitting, taking food parcels and some drinks to the men on duty over the Christmas period who spent their turn on board Light Vessels.

Mr and Mrs Tim Webster, lady and gentleman, Mr Webster being a regular chairman of Clacton Council, held in great esteem by all Lifeboat Cox'n's and crew members, plus L.V. Masters and Crew members, Sailing Barge Masters and Crew alike. These most honest folk dedicated their lives to men of the sea and it was my honour and privilege to know personally these most remarkable people and most of the sailormen I have written about. The late Mrs Webster, with her life dedicated to men of the sea, at Christmas time in the middle 1960's had a most tragic ending whilst preparing to attend the R.N.L.I. Dinner and Dance. Her body was taken by Lifeboat and crew and buried at sea, which she so loved.

A. A. Jefferies of Brightlingsea, who was over 80 years of age in 1923, being a Lloyds Shipping agent for 45 years faithful service. His father had been through life a Master Mariner in sailing ships; he was a Smack owner and the cottage in the High Street, Brightlingsea, was within the Jefferies family for over 100 years. There were 10 to 15 apprentice lads living in the attic rooms and dwellings at the rear of this fantastically built house. The lads were brilliant seamen, many became Master Mariners and most had come from the Poor Houses and Institutes of Colchester. The same as the 10 to 15 lads at a time residing in our family (Brasteds) home at No. 91 High Street Local. These lads were found in food and clothing and received, if they were lucky, a few shillings spending money to enjoy themselves at the grand fair on arrival to our Cinque Port Town of Brightlingsea twice a year.

A. A. Jefferies was apprenticed to his father, working on board our family boats and cultivating oysters upon our family freehold tidal plots. Tidal plots of which numbered many in the North and South Channel in and around Underwoods Hard, Lynche Creek and many tidal plots above leading to Flag Creek, where members of the Jefferies family resided at Hill Cottage. Working our tidal plots and ground rights freehold ground and 1000-year Royal Charter leasehold ground rights, of which, 200 years on many of our family ground rights have not expired. A. A. Jefferies fished in the North Sea, he later in life became Secretary to the Smack Owners Association and was an author writer historian, recording mostly all local shipping tragedies and disasters at sea of our fisherfolk heroes of the sea.

These brave fishermen, most courageous mariners wherever they hailed from or sailed upon, they were and still are the fishermen most brave mariners, with sometimes reaping a good harvest of fish from the sea, with that same selfish sea reaping a good harvest of heroic fisherman in return. Our local fisherman were known and respected as Swin Rangers and were all God-fearing men and thought little of running under sail through the swin in Easterly or North Easterly gales, when the only lights to be seen were the sunk Light Vessel at the seaward end and the Nore Light Ship at the other. Our fishermen carried out some gallant rescues of shipwrecked passengers and crew members, saving thousands of lives and in most cases their heroic deeds of bravery were inadequately rewarded.

During the March 1883 hurricane which swept across England, we lost 20 of our local sailormen; fishermen who perished on board fishing craft SV Recruit, SV Smack Conquest and the Lugger Mascotte, making 20 children fatherless overnight from the Cinque Port Town of Brightlingsea. With the sad loss of our three Brightlingsea boats, lost off the Dutch Coast off Horkom. On that very same month almost 500 children had been made fatherless overnight from the larger fishing ports such as Aberdeen, Grimsby, Fleetwood, Shields, Lowestoft and Yarmouth, and all sea ports with their stories of the sea to tell.

In the year 1883, thanks to Squire Bateman and his lady wife and the Reverend Arthur Pertwee, who acted like ministering angels, fifty widows in all and 20 children had been dependent of those mariners who were called to Higher Circles through the gale, but thanks to the effort of Mr Egerton Green, plus the committee members of the Stock Exchange and Lloyds shipping, all were adequately provided for.

In January 1894 the most brave and gallant Cox'n of the R.N.L.I. of Clacton-on-Sea, William Scofield, was awarded a Silver Medal by the King of Denmark. He had previously received one from the French President and the Medal of the Royal Lifeboat Institution. I am very much indebted to the late Mrs Meg Bollingbroke, who sadly passed away in August 1992, and son Rod, for kindness shown to my works and writings with the help of photographs in memory of dearest Charles Bollingbroke, who served a term of office as Cox'n of the Clacton Lifeboat and of all the men who went down to the sea in ships and did their works in dangerous hours and troubled waters.

November 1992, tribute to Sailing Barge Master late Bill Gorf of Sittingbourne, Kent. As one journeys through life, one learns more every day and as we approach once again November, when we should one and all not only in November, but remember our heroes and our loved ones, friends and relatives at all times, friend and foe alike, being some mother's son whom fell in battle. Just recently I have had the pleasure to meet a gentleman, Mr Luther Gorf, of Sittingbourne, Kent, by chance whose maritime father recorded his daily routine by log (Cargo Book), for the years 1940, 1941 and 1942 with far too much detail to have all of his works entered into these chapters.

As follows:

1940 - 9th February: Booked on Dole, ordered to lay by the Henry Jabez, sunk at Queensborough.

Tuesday 10th February: Came down, someone took our boat, they are fighting the Germans, but there are people in England worse than Germans.

Friday 13th September: Got to Albert Dock, could not dock, walked up to Rawks Mills, nothing but devastation all the way from North Woolwich. Rows of houses down and warehouses burnt, can't get anything for next week, as the Mills have been burnt. Two Air Raids in the day, another lasting all night. Late Skipper Bill Gorf, a man with love of fellow man.

Saturday. 14th May, 1941: Quiet night this way, several warnings, dogfights in afternoon. Warning 10.55 pm, any amount of planes going over. Saw three come down in flames, a bit hot all round, looks as if London is getting it bad.

Sunday, May: Heard someone shouting about 1.30, could not make it out, saw a man on the sea-wall 2.20am. Went over to him, found it was a Gerry, he put his hands up, took his revolver from him and put him in the boat. Took him aboard, found he was wounded in the head and in pain in the groin. He was wet through, took his clothes off, gave him a cup of Cocoa and put him in my bunk. Fired 12 Very lights for Police, none came before 9am. Very quiet chap and about 24 years old, could not see him in pain and wet through. If I had left him be where he was, the rats would have had him, it was a question for Sid Walker what would you do? He had 3 thousand French Francs, 900 -100 Franc Notes, 1-50 1-20, and 8 Francs in Belgian Money. Name in hat: Huter Richard.

It could be viable that this German airman is still alive. I might just find out someday.

During the Second World War the Trinity House Light Vessel Service played an important role to do their utmost to safeguard shipping from maritime tragedies, and the Trinity House Light Vessel Service, Steam Vessel tender. Ex Steam Vessel Miranda in 1940 was mastered by a gentleman from the Isle of Wight, named Captain McCarthy, with the first officer, who was highly respected on board ship and was nicknamed Socks Harris. This is known through never wearing his socks.

Mr Harris became a serving master on board Trinity House Vessels and who was later promoted to Superintendent. Mr Victor Potter, born and bred from Tollesbury, Essex, residing at Dovercourt, a retired mariner, he was a Second World War yachtsman, with many years to his credit as a serving seaman with the Trinity House Service. A man, along with his lady wife, who showed much kindness when I visited their warm and friendly home. Their son is a chief engineer at sea. His late maritime father, Charles William Potter, yachtsman, fisherman and a man who served the Royal Navy during the First World War, Royal Navy being R.N.V.R. He was awarded the Distinguished Service Medal for bravery at sea.

Mr Potter, to whom I myself had the pleasure to

know personally from my childhood and manhood days. Knowing this sailorman from the good old days when brilliant mariners of Tollesbury and Wivenhoe arrived in our local creek, with fish, sprats and lovely clean shrimps. We had several buyer managers for various companies.

Mr Bert Durrant, a man who at the age of 16 years advanced his age and fought on the battlefields of France. He also served deep sea as seaman with Blue Funnel Line. Mr Durrant was buyer manager for Tabor. In the good old days, our local mariners could earn sixpence per hour. In the winter months, when there were no fish, they earnt no money; the locals respected the Day brothers, they would transport many of the sprats with their lovely tumbrils and carts.

The late Bert Clark, a most jovial man, drove Jack Osbourne's Bedford lorry, registration number FTW 51, through one of my fairly wealthy relatives who took bribes from 3 Tollesbury-smack owners, to purchase their fish first on arrival to the creek. This man's wife had a one hundred guinea piano purchased for her. This is how Tollesbury became known as Piano Junction

Charles William Potter of Tollesbury, Distinguished Service Medal, Royal Navy, R.N.V.R. A grand yachtsman and fisherman. He served as a ship's watchkeeper, when 32 ships were laid up in the River Blackwater.

I myself was involved with all ships for a livelihood at the same time. World famous Captain Ned Heard, with nerves of steel, sadly died on board ship in 1947 whilst taken ill, being a perfect gentleman whom I had known and greatly respected from man and boy. With the same respects shown to his son, Ted Heard Junior, of Tollesbury, a 1930 Shamrock sailorman and a 1937 Endeavour crew member.

Back to the First World War - Brightlingsea. Our forgotten local heroes, many who had returned back to their native home, returning from America to fight for freedom and democracy.

The following details are founded on facts and I find it a must to record these writings and recordings for the sake of humanity. Dad and his shipmates who had all been serving the gentry folk. Greatly respected members of the Vanderbilt's family on board their luxury yachts serving and sailing in America - Steam Yacht Warrior and Steam Yacht Vanadis, N.Y.Y.C.

Our local mariners, my father A. Jefferies, Snap Walter Everett, Bumper Everett, Sap Gilbert, Mr Joe Richardson, Senior, Mr Jim and Charles Goodwin, Senior, George Peggs, Senior, Ernie Dido Smith, Noble Field, Luther Gould and Jeff Dines, Senior, they were only home for two days, when one and all volunteered along with 100 local yachting lads to join the Rifle Brigade, not forgetting his shipmates and battle friends F. Ruffell and B. Hasted. Lord Kitchener's army went straight off to a bloody war. They had joined up in the old local Foresters Hall, and were shipped out of Dover with their training, battle-drill and rifle training carried out on board ship. Foresters Hall is owned by a brilliant sailmaker, Mr Jim Lawrence, who was a Barge sailorman as a young lad, the same as Mr Sid Westwood and Mr Peter Powell.

With Dad in battle were mariners Bill Gilders, Senior, Ted Woods, Senior, whose son is a retired yacht master, a gentleman who resides in Southampton. A yacht master, Bill Goodwin, was made a Captain on the battlefield. Jack Handley, Junior, was also made a Captain on the battlefield, being the son of fearless skipper Jack Handley, Senior, a Shamrock sailorman and a hardman but a most kind man who showed kindness during my youth.

Skipper Jack Handley, during the winter months skippered down the channel for Mr Poole, who was superintendent of the River Police and many hardened local skippers served these vessels during the winter months, to go down channel scalloping, including mariners Big Harry Cole, Big George Rickwood, Big Sid Martin, Big Charlie Death, who was a Cape Horn square rig sailorman and a close neighbour. He was also a navigator serving the Royal racing cutter Britannia in 1904 and 1910 racing seasons, with all old photographs in my keeping.

Mariner skipper Big Bill Gunn was an uncle of my much respected friend Mr William Gunn of Local, a pleasant man until upset. As a young man he spent much of his time fishing off Iceland, on board Lowestoft trawlers. These mariners mentioned were known and respected as giants of men and had the most powerful great strength. Also serving escalloping were most jovial mariners, Walter Pittick, Skipper Barney Beere and Mr Barnard. Sailorman Barney was a most kind man, who would sit all night at times to keep his dying shipmates on shore company in their hours of need. Sadly, Jack Handley, Junior, drowned from Steam Vessel Orient on leaving Ramsgate Harbour in the bad weather of March 1926. Most sadly this mariner has no tile upon the fringe of All Saints Church wall to remember him by.

Back to the First World War. With Dad in battle was a jovial farm worker, ploughman and horseman, Fred King, who was awarded for bravery the

Distinguished Service Order. Also in battle was Charlie Blye, serving the Rifle Brigade. A ship and yacht painter during the fierce and bloody battle of Ypres. Also serving was Reg Gilders of late, who was shot through the arm and was also gassed. Mr Gilders was a most jovial respected man, A ship's painter by trade, and enameller; a good living man who worked in Aldous shipyard for many years. During my youth when we had 750 men, women and lads, clocked in for manual Admiralty work everyday in the local Aldous shipyard, of which is still the gateway to the world where certain councillors only classed this priceless waterfront as a burden to the town and rate-payers. It was sold off in too much haste with no foreseeable future: however, I do not intend to enter into local politics. Also in battle with Dad and his comrades was T. Bragg serving the Rifle Brigade who most sadly died, aged 30 years, from his Ypres war wounds, registration number Z1281, 15th December 1919 - gone but not forgotten. Jim Goodwin was at sea and in battle with Dad, and Mr Goodwin died aged 69 years on 24th May 1959. Mr and Mrs Goodwin and family lost their lovable son at sea, William Herbert Goodwin, on D-Day, 6th June 1944, Royal Navy fighting for freedom. Mr Jim Goodwin owned CK Foxhound. Noble field in battle with Dad and at sea owned CK Ethel Emily. My lovable cousin, Leslie A. Jefferies, sadly drowned serving the Royal Navy from H.M.S. Crested Eagle in bad weather, and was laid to rest in Gillingham Naval Cemetery in 1942.

Luther Gould who was killed in battle at Ypres in France.

Dad was still with most of his shipmates come army pals until his capture at Ypres on 3rd September 1916 in France, when he was taken Prisoner of War. Comrades mentioned in my works, their awards were made for their bravery in the face of their enemy, who were also most brave and most courageous German soldiers and, like our soldiers, being all some mothers' sons.

Dad spoke but little of his vast experience of life spent at sea and in battle. Dad and his comrades had taken over a stronghold and had fought bloody hard in the face of their enemy to retrieve the keys from the stronghold point, sadly killing many good soldiers. Jack Handley, Junior, was the first soldier to retrieve the keys and he also received, along with my father, shell shock for their heroism!

When Luther Gould became shot and wounded and blown to pieces in a detonated minefield, my father crawled upon his hands and knees into this minefield to retrieve a text prayer-book from the tunic pocket of his closest friend Luther Gould who lay dead - blown to pieces, at the young age of 21 years. This was a promise Dad had made to Luther's parents.

Mrs Phylis Gould who died on 7th November 1934 aged 67 years.

IA 714850

(Printed by authority of the Registrar-General.)

D. Cert.
R.B.D.

The Statutory Fee for this Certificate is 2s. 7d. If required subsequently to registration, a Search Fee is payable in addition.

CERTIFIED COPY of an ENTRY OF DEATH.
Pursuant to the Births and Deaths Registration Acts, 1836 to 1929.

Registration District Tendring

1934. Death in the Sub-district of Ardleigh in the County of Essex

Insert in this Margin any Notes which appear in the original entry.

Columns:— 1		2	3	4	5	6	7	8	9
No.	When and where Died.	Name and Surname.	Sex.	Age.	Rank or Profession.	Cause of Death	Signature, Description, and Residence of Informant.	When Registered.	Signature of Registrar.
104	Sixth November 1934 44 Upper Park Road Brightlingsea U.D.	Phyllis Gould	Female	64 years	Widow of Luther Martin Gould a Master Mariner	1(a) Cardiac Failure (b) Carcinomes of Intestines No P.M. Certified by Kenneth E. Bury L.R.C.P.	R. W. Gould Son Present at the death 24 Lower Park Road Brightlingsea	Seventh November 1934	B. A. Stevens Registrar.

I, Stanley Alexander Stevens, Registrar of Births and Deaths for the Sub-District of Ardleigh, in the County of Essex do hereby certify that this is a true copy of the Entry No. 104 in the Register Book of Deaths for the said Sub-District, and that such Register Book is now legally in my custody.

WITNESS MY HAND this Seventh day of November, 1934.

Registrar of Births and Deaths.

CAUTION.—Any person who (1) falsifies any of the particulars on this Certificate, or (2) uses it as true, knowing it to be falsified, is liable to Prosecution under the Forgery Act, 1913.

Captain Luther Gould, Senior, was a Master Mariner, in the art of sail - a gentleman. (He was the proprietor of the lovely old Cherry Tree Public House local, during the First World War, until his death in 1925, along with his lady wife Phyllis who died in her Lower Park home in 1934). On the outbreak of the war Mr and Mrs Gould held a most strong premonition that their son would be killed in battle, and my father had denied orders to retreat by his commanding officers and shipmates mentioned in my story.

The most kind respected German Commandant ordered his troops not to fire their rifles at Dad, and in perfect English he explained to Dad the best way how to escape from a most dangerous predicament and out of the detonated minefield. Dad, nearing God's call, told quietly how he respected the most kind German Commandant. Upon being captured this German gentleman, in perfect English, said: "You are a most courageous friend and a fighting true soldier, a much loyal friend", and after examining the text prayer-book, he passed it back to Dad and said: "Well, my good brave man, you are now a Prisoner of War and I pray to God you are able to fulfil your promise to your friend's parents", and Dad most certainly did. This sacred possession is still safe-guarded within the Gould family to this day. With the treasured photographs within the prayer book of Captain Luther Gould, a famous sailing master, his lady wife Phyllis and a photograph of Luther, Junior. He was sadly killed in battle, fighting with local lads at Ypres in France aged 21 years on 3rd September 1916. This story is based on gospel facts, God bless their memory, British and Germans alike. It most certainly is not only just the Nazis who try to destroy knowledge in my case.

Many grand mariners came into my life and as a lad, after Aldous shipyard days, during the Second World War, I worked with the late Mr G. G. Holland, a plumber and a friend whose maritime father had sailed the world deep sea with 10 full seasons to his credit, as foc'sle cook along with late Bill Blackwood of Wivenhoe on board the Royal racing cutter Britannia. Mr G. G. Holland, was named after his grandfather George Gilbert, who lost his young life at sea during the 1883 North Sea gales. Being a brother of Captain Robert Gilbert, a famous local yacht master, who lived to reach a grand age of 105 years - died 18th january 1958.

During my youth and working on board Motor Vessel Native with many mariners who had sailed the world, Mr Jack Francis was foreman of the river for Colchester Corporation and has sailed as mariner on board Flying Cloud in 1922-23, and many famous yachts including Schooner Sona, owned by Miss Betty Carstairs, U.S.A.

Roy Griggs, world travelled sailorman, Royal Naval Reservist, and a true friend, was also on board Native. During his time at sea, during the First World War, his treasured son Derek, aged 7 years, was tragically killed by a naval lorry near the local cinema, which is now the Doctor's Surgery. Sadly, the naval ship Mr Griggs was serving on board was due to sail out of Portsmouth and sadly he was not permitted compassionate leave.

Skipper Roy Griggs skippered during the early 1950's the sea-going Motor Yacht, MY Waterwitch, which was owned by Maxwell Reid and the fabulous actress Joan Collins from the days when they spent much time in Brightlingsea.

Mariner late George Bragg, a much respected sailorman, was also working on board the Motor Vessel Native, as a freeman of the River Colne, this being our Royal Charter birthright, Mr Bragg was one of three survivors when the Duke of Bedford's 1,400 ton Steam Yacht, SY Sapphire, Royal Yacht Squadron, serving under the Admiralty during the First World War, when this magnificent yacht struck two mines off the entrance of Shannack Dardanelles and sank in seven minutes with much loss of life! 78 officers and ratings in all. Mr Bragg ran from for'd to aft, wearing no lifejacket and he went down with the ship, under the water. He prayed for God to save his life and his prayer was answered as he appeared from under the sea. His hands came down upon a floating hatch board and God had answered his prayer.

Mr Bragg's brother, Ridgeway Bragg, G. Salmon, W. T. Steady and SubLieutenant Doyle, were lost off Cromarty on 24th February 1917 from H.M. Patrol Yacht SS Varona under the Admiralty, along with John Burgess Everett, who perished aged 59 years on 25th September 1915 from SS Sandra off Zeebrugge; he was the grandfather of my school-pal, Mr John Everett whose grandmother was a close neighbour. Mr Bragg's jovial brother of late, Captain William Bragg, was senior master in Everards Coasting Vessels, serving many years, and their father, who was a world travelled sailorman, and a Cape Horn sailorman, was serving on board a British barquentine in America, on the day Jessie James was shot in the back on 3rd April 1882. Mr George Bragg was almost 90 years of age when he passed away. His son John and I had served yachting together on board MY Virginia Mediterranean cruising. John's brother Tony is a well versed world travelled marine engineer, a retired deep seaman. A sea that can be so kind and so ruthless. It is all sacred memories from the past.

Mr William Bragg, mariner aged 85 years, in 1941 was still working and collecting oysters, along with mariners B. Jefferies and A. Jefferies. Mariners who had served the mammoth Shamrocks as seamen, and my old photographs show these mariners working upon our Royal Charter tidal plots in the South Channel. These mariners, being my great uncles whom along with my grandfather Edward, whose son-in-law was the world famous Captain Robert Wringe.

Within my maritime history book, I find it a must to pay tribute to gentleman Mr Les Kemble, Funeral Director of Wivenhoe, to whom I have known and greatly respected for many years. With this quiet gentleman having the greatest respect towards my lifetime's works. The late sailorman, Harry Field and his charming wife, Rosie, being uncle and auntie to Mr Kemble, and all folk in our town respected Mr and Mrs Field, as our maritime community was one time a bond of honour. Sailorman Harry was indeed a regular serving seaman on board the Royal racing cutter Britannia, and the mastheadsman, whilst working aloft during bad weather and racing, by sheer accident dropped his marlin spike and this knocked Mr Field's right eye out of his head and onto the deck. Mrs Field, a lady whom was a family friend and who was called Auntie Rosie, was totally blind, an extremely kind lady. Auntie Rosie, as we respectfully called this grand lady, not once did she complain of what nature had deprived her; of her precious eyesight and she always said, "at least my Harry and I have got one eye between us both". Mrs Field made and baked the most delicious cakes and made lovely homemade wine.

As I sit with my pen in hand, midday 5th January 1995, writing my memoirs and maritime history book, the second best Bible on the book shelves in the world today. For decent folk with a true love of our heritage and for the memory of our loved ones who are no longer with us and are no longer upon God's earth.

Sailorman Vic Potter, at the young age of 20 years in 1940, was a serving seaman on board Steam Vessel Vesta, ex-Steam Vessel Miranda. During the time of the war with the ship being attacked off the Nabb Tower by enemy aircraft fire. Sailorman the late Bloss Ford from East Cowes, Isle of Wight, was a Boer War soldier and he was shot through the cheeks of his backside whilst standing in the wash-room. Many bombs exploded alongside of the ship and the engines moved from their beds. The ship was powered by twin reciprocating engines and the vessel could steam at 18 knots, with 30 odd serving officers and crew members.

Captain Harris, nicknamed the Deck Lad, aged 20 years. Mr Vic Potter, the Dean of Tollesbury, had sailed as shipmates with my shore-going pals fishermen, yachtsmen from Port Isaac - late Jack Richards, late Fred Honey, and late Ned Stevens. Sailormen who were picked up by the Admiralty from serving yachting. These mariners being Royal Naval Reservists who had to report for naval duty upon the first day of the Second World War. These sailormen with Mr Potter and his maritime father were serving on board the 90-ton Ketch Yacht, Royal Yacht Squadron, code number M.N.N.W. The highly respected gentleman owner was Captain Arthur Grenville Soames of the Blues and Greys Regiment. His son, the late Lord Christopher Soames, was married to Lady Mary Churchill, whose grandson is Nicholas Soames, M.P.

In 1939, yacht Dawn Star was mastered by late

Captain Arthur Grenville Soames at the wheel of S.Y. Dawn Star R.Y.S.

Captain Hedgely of Southampton. The mate was late Charles William Potter of Tollesbury. A man named Dimmick from Southampton was the cook. Sailors from Port Isaac were my shore-going pals from my own yachting career, Ned Stevens, Fred Honey, wrestler Andrew Steer and strong-man John Mills. These most jovial mariners resided close by my own good shipmates Fred and Frank Grills, Dan Mutton, Jack Spry, Little Morley, Dick Stevens - mariners, friends and shipmates. Dan Mutton served as Bosun of Shamrock V in 1930 and he also served as Bosun of Endeavour in 1937.

With all the facts and household names and all photographs in my main story, and also many photographs of owner and crew members leaving Arcachon in the Bay of Biscay just prior to the Second World War. Mostly all Port Isaac mariners were reservists and most were picked up by the Admiralty when all folks' contented way of life was sadly disrupted.

The luxury Steam Yacht Conqueror was owned by gentry folk of Selfridges. Gordon Selfridge was a most caring gentleman towards fellow man and was a Director of the Royal Mailship Steamship SS Titanic Fund H.M.S. Conqueror came under T124 Articles during the Second World War and was under the command of Captain E. R. T. Chambers, Royal Navy, of Southampton, who was Captain and Commander of Operations.

Lieutenant Butler Clayton Bromwell with an engine room compliment greatly respected from Southampton. A few Southampton seamen recalled; Sid and Frank Ballard, Harry Bushall, boatswain, Reg Bushall and Charlie Smith. Some Asdic ratings, Stuart Smith from Glasgow, George Fry from London. Southampton stokers Harry Thorpe, Ted White, Snowy White, T. Furmage, M. Morgan. Mariners of local who were serving seamen in line of duty, Charlie Goodwin, Junior, who resides in Australia, Cyril Jefferies - dad's cousin, George King, Junior, known as Prunie, son of Fred King. Fred King, during the First World War was awarded the Distinguished Service Order for bravery in the face of the enemy. Ted Wood, Neville Wood, Adrian Wood, George Peggs - nicknamed Knocker - he was a shipmate of my maritime father who, along with Mr Charles Branch, including Charles Hempstead respected natives of our town. Charles Branch being R.N. during the Second World War and a retired Customs Officer. My father and these mentioned sailormen raced on board Sunbeam II in Canada in 1937 and won the "Round the Island" race under Captain Nicholas, an A1 sailorman.

H.M.S. Conqueror carried on board experts from America for the training of Asdic ratings, serving from Southampton to Portland with 28 rocket launching pads on board ship; this is a known recorded fact. The H.M.S. Conqueror and her gallant officers and crew members had brought down into the sea three enemy aircraft.

My work that has taken sixty years of my life with knowledge, plus a lifetime's collection of priceless archive material. With over 20 years to compile my lifetime's works, of which regrettably, have all so far been unrecognised by many professionals and societies with the BBC broadcasting on many occasions. Our heritage is a most sacred treasured possession, and for what our gallant sailormen did for our country I sincerely trust it is not asking too much to have them one and all remembered all the time.

Last and not just once per year at the Cenotaph, if not for my sake but for their sake and their respected families, who fought for freedom, and most of all for the sake of humanity, as no man upon God's earth, unsponsored and unrecognised for over 22 years, could have worked harder in their sacred memory. No man could ask for more.

My lifetime's works are fully cross referenced with the great cities of Gosport, Southampton, Cornwall and Essex.

Bayard Brown, the eccentric American millionaire, who died on board his magnificent steam yacht Valfreyia in 1926, with the full unpublished facts and photographs within my main stories. Captain George Pennick of Brightlingsea married a Miss Puice Thrower prior to the Second World War, making their home in Southampton. Captain George Pennick, serving the Royal Navy, served on board this luxury yacht under the Admiralty during the Second World War and he was shot dead, whilst standing upon the foc'sle head, by enemy aircraft fire. Captain Pennick was buried in the city of Southampton with full naval honours in a ceremonial parade, with many Admiralty dignitaries in attendance from Portsmouth Command. And another one of our gallant sailormen of Brightlingsea was laid to rest.

1939 Owner and crew members, serving on board yacht Dawn Star. Gentleman owner Captain Arthur Grenville Soames.

1932 Owners of Schooner Yacht Radiant Ex Xarifa N.Y.Y.C.
Owners Lord and Lady Iliffe - Newspaper Tycoon.

Xarifa was built and launched by Whites (Samuel Whites) of Cowes I.O.W. 1930.
All the facts and household names are within the JJ Photography Collection.

Late Friend Ted Heard of Tollesbury Died 17/2/99 Aged 93	Late Len Riley 2nd Steward	Kenhoe West Cornwell	Mr King Chief Steward Southampton	Arthur Thomas Port Isaac West Cornwell	Late Friend Cyril Coates of Tollesbury Died 17/7/98 Aged 86
Gerry Sweet Port Isacc Standing Boat Swain	Mr Lloyd Chief Engineer Southampton	Friend Phil Williams Died Summer 85 Aged 78	Mr Hoskins Port Isaac	Percy Howe Brightlingsea	Mr Sibley 2nd Engineer South
Tony Wilsmore Tollesbury	Clive Stokes of Tollesbury Southampton 3rd Mate	Jack Coyde Chef Southampton	Captain Fred Stokes of Tollesbury Home Southampton	Mr Tweed 1st Mate Brilliant Navigator Scotland	Jim Lewis Tollesbury 2nd Cook

The brilliant 2nd Mate - Mr Durham, held his Extra Master's Qualifications Aged 24 years.
His maritime father was greatly respected. He also mastered S.Y. Albion.

Sailormen Ted Heard, Cyril Coates and Phil Williams were serving members on board Endeavours in 1937.

ROYAL RACING CUTTER BRITANNIA & THE FAMOUS SCHOONER WESTWARD

These were two of the most famous racing machines of all times and the other famous yachts are all mentioned within the JJ stories including all the masters and the mariners, household names of the sailormen of Great Britain.

The Royal Racing Cutter Britannia carried, over the years, many in crew Mr. Joe Giles from Cowes, IOW, proudly served as 1st mate on her too. My late maritime father sailed on many great yachts, Iolanda, Tuscarora and the rest. But sailing on board 24 metre Lulworth & Sapphire II, he found the late Capt. Stan Gilbert and his grand crew were among the best. There was Billy Austin (local) and Sam Thomas (Port Isaac), both of late, and Len Diaper and Bill Braden, from the river Itchen. I knew well these sailors great. In 1952, Bill Braden at the age of 76 sailed with me I was only a young lad at the time, at the age of 23. Bill was as tough as old leather, and a damn good pal. He had spent long hours at sea as by the look on his face, one could tell. He was a tardy mariner, and so very kind. Not a more honest sailorman could anyone find. As, one of his regular Captains was equally as tough. As, without a guard-rail he sailed, even when the weather was rough. Sporting his gold teeth and an earring, and with a cigar under steam. He was always smartly dressed in his yachting suit and polished boots that did gleam. He never worried about storms, with heavy seas and a swell. And to my dear friend Bill Braden, Capt. Len Evans from the River Itchen was his best pal. I have compiled records of all of the old sailors, complete with photos as well. With regard to trying to obtain recognition - it's like trying to scull a boat out of hell! The good Lord up above knows I am honest and a good, honest publisher I seek. I'm sure those good mariners up above, often look down, for a peep. Capt. Donald McKillopp, a very nice gent, whom I personally knew, too Commanded M.Y. Phillante when it was brand new. In 1937, he steamed out to Endeavours I & II and possess all of the photos I have quite a few. It is a pleasure, and a privilege, to say I knew many of the crew. It is still a great pleasure to socialise with the remaining few, Only last Christmas, I received Xmas cards through my door. They came from surviving mariners - no man could ask for more.

My good sailorman friend, the late Ted Heard of Tollesbury, the son of the famous Captain Ned Heard. Ted sailed on board as the ships carpenter in 1930 on board Shamrock V and also on Endeavour in 1937 and he was called to rest 17th February 1999, aged 93 years. I was proud to be able to attend his funeral service.

As previously stated within my maritime recordings it was also a very sad day in my life, being much involved with the laid up shipping on the River Blackwater, when most sadly Captain Ned Heard was taken ill on board ship and sadly died. A fitting farewell to a man of the sea, a Master of the Sea who proved his seamanship on the homeward voyage, with the help of the navigator and brilliant crewmembers. This, when Endeavour was on her homeward voyage October 1937, arriving home, in Portsmouth, to a heroes welcome. The Master and the crew wished only to get home to their loved ones.

MY VIRGINIA RYS

UNDER THE COMMAND OF THE LATE CAPTAIN BEHENNA OF ST. IVES, CORNWALL, (HOME SOUTHAMPTON)

In the photograph above are two of the regular serving crewmembers. J. Jefferies and Tom Martin of Southampton, shipmate and friend being ex Royal Navy 2nd World War submariner. Tom & I were most proud of the fact that whilst serving on board this fabulous luxury yacht which was a fine sea vessel, cruising untold mileage under the ownership of gentleman Lord Viscount and Lady Camrose of the Daily Telegraph. Our respected owner departed this life on God's earth in June 1954.

In the year 1951 MY Virginia was chartered for 6 months by gentry folk, Duke & Duchess of Westminster. We cruised inside the Arctic Circle and Lapland as far as Bossekop, well inside the land of the midnight sun where the Duke of Westminster much enjoyed his favourite sport of salmon fishing.

MY Virginia was built in Scotland in 1930 for Lord Courtauld, company silk manufacturer, and director. Captain Arthur Bishop first mastered the yacht and the 1st mate serving was Captain Robert Wringe, jnr who was my maritime father's cousin. The serving boatswain was J. Fletcher of Liskard, Cornwall. The Chief engineer was Les Bishop, local. The chief steward was Ron Summers who, along with his brother Arthur were nephews of the famous Captain Arthur Bishop, master mariner. Arthur Summers, at almost 96 years young a most jovial gentlemen, a pre-war yachtsman, he started his yachting career at the age of fourteen years on board SY Rosabelle at the end of the First World War. Most of the mariners of whom I have written are no longer upon God's earth and for the sake of humanity and their families my writings and recordings are in sacred memory of all the gentry folk and remarkable yacht owners, masters and our sailormen.

During my youth as a lad in Aldous Shipyard during the Second World War, when there were 740 men, women and lads clocking in each day for Admiralty work, mariner Fred Brooks would always have a go at me being small and frail at the time. He would grab a hold of me and stick his teeth into me. One day, my father was coming ashore with Nunkie Noble Field and Jeff Dines. They had returned from the Colne on board steam tug Bricklesea, after tendering the naval craft. Fred Brooks was enjoying another feed and had just said my family would starve on you there being more meat on a butcher's apron. Just as my father and his friends were approaching, dad asked me what the hell it was all about and being wet behind the ears at the time I told dad. He got a hold of poor old skipper Brooks and bit his ear and said: "You eat our family and I will bloody turn cannibal long enough to eat yours"; dad and Fred both being tough old seamen through life. Several weeks later, skipper Fred gave me a harmonica and his uncle Ned's bronze medal which he had won racing in Ostend on board a yacht with his name on. But in all honesty, I regretfully parted with it to a friend. Skipper Fred and I became friends and I know that both him and dad knew how far they could go with each other. The lad Jim Frost of Tollesbury was to join Mignonette but was taken ill and did not sail. His photograph still hangs on a family wall in Tollesbury.

The crew of the Mignonette, yawl rigged, was built by Robbie Aldous and Robbie Rashbrook for Thomas Hall in 1867. It was 52 ft. in length, 7.4 ft. draught and was originally skippered by Captain B. Chaplain of Brightlingsea and the court hearings on the charge was kept very brief; their life story not entering much into the summing up. Captain Dudley and mate Edwin Stevens, Edward Brooks and deck boy Richard Parker of the River Itchen. Richard being a younger son of a widow and had been semi-adopted by the good Captain Matthews and his good lady wife and the Parker family, remaining constantly kind to young Richard. The Matthews family River Itchen many in numbers and famous yachting masters.

Well the little yawl departed from Tollesbury in May 1884 and sailed round for Southampton, calling in at Shoreham on her way. Captain Dudley tried hard to persuade his brother William to make the voyage on board the Mignonette. When the yacht left Tollesbury with the view of sailing on a run job to Sydney, Australia, the job went begging and the most brilliant local seafarers thought how stupid it was not to have such a small vessel shipped out. It was not as such a new owner seeking adventure and the task was laughed out of Tollesbury. However, the proof is always in the pudding where fools fear to tread. The Mignonette struck bad weather by sunrise on 5th July; it was estimated that the yacht was approximately 1,500 miles from the Cape of Good Hope when a heavy sea struck her and stowed her starboard side clean in. Allowing no time for preparation she heeled over and sunk. The crew had to abandon her and it is a known fact a good clinker-built 13 ft. dingy handled with care would likely starve you before drowning you. So with very little food and even less water they managed to climb into the small boat taking the boat cover with them. The yacht and dinghy were both built by the brilliant shipwright's Robbie Aldous and Robbie Rashbrook and after the storm moderated, they made and jury rigged up a small sail and steered by oar. Captain Dudley was most fortunate to quickly get hold of his sextant and the compass. A terrible ordeal was in front of them and for the next 24 days their skillful seamanship, comradeship and hardship was put to the test. They were most fortunate to have their oilskins on when disaster struck and with these and the boat cover it gave them some shelter from the raging deep and the boiling hot sun. They managed to catch a small turtle some days later after the storm and saved some fresh water from a squall, but in the tropics it is best to drink it up before the sun dries it up. After 19 days of torment and suffering with no water and no food, it was stated in the Assizes that Captain Dudley had decided to draw lots to see who should die for the others to survive. Poor little Richard did not have any say in the matter; he was too weak and all the decisions were made by Captain Dudley. It was said they drew lots and it was said the youngest and weakest in the open boat had to be murdered for food. I have never in my life played God's judge and jury on another person's life and their choice between life and death must have been an agonising decision. It is very difficult trying to imagine making such a decision. These poor souls must have suffered - they could have decided to quietly slip over the side but it was decided that Captain Dudley would kill little Richard; and this was quickly and quietly done by Captain Dudley with his knife. Richard being to ill and weak to realise and his body was ripped open and three men ate heartily at his heart and liver. Prior to this incident, Ned Brooks cried and prayed to God for Captain Dudley not to kill the lad, but this had been on his mind for some considerable time.

On 28th July 1884 aboard the German Barque Montezuma, Captain Simonsen was bound from Rio de Janeiro to Hamburg and had sailed out of a seaport of southern Chile. It was Ned Brooks who first sighted the vessel and this gave the three survivors hope. They kept the small boat on course and managing to row the boat owing to the fact that their strength had built up from devouring little Richard. The barque spotted them and took the men aboard. They had sailed almost 1,000 miles from where the Mignonette foundered and when rescued by the Montezuma they were 1,000 miles from the Brazilian coast. They were given medical attention. Captain Dudley had no intention of getting rid of Richard's body until he made doubly sure it was a ship, as he wished to make sure he could keep his fresh supply of human flesh. Not only had murder been committed but cannibalism also, but the dinghy with Richard's remains laying in the bottom was hoisted aboard. The Captain, after a post-mortem was carried out had the body sewn up in canvas and they had a service over his body before committing it to the deep on 16th September 1884. The Montezuma sailed into Falmouth and the survivors were landed. The small boat was taken ashore by the Customs and Police to be held as evidence and the crew were taken into custody, pending a murder enquiry. Under the jurisdiction of the mayor and 7 magistrates the crew were found guilty of murder and served six months in prison without hard labour. The small boat was on exhibition in Cornwall for many years.

MIGNONETTE RICHARD PARKER POETRY

Look out Jefferies Boy, here I come
Take out my knife, have slices off your bum,
Cut them up into little slices,
Not much enjoyment without any spices.
If your little relation was as small as you,
This must have been the reason of Captain Dudley,
Cutting him up to chew.
After being wrecked in the Mignonette
The proper type of food they all had to forget.
They ate it in the dark without any gravy
After 19 days adrift in the open boat.
All crew wished they had joined the Royal Navy.
Captain Dudley cut out his heart and he cut out his liver.
This made my poor old uncle Ned, shudder and shiver.
Poor little Richard Parker did not ask to die
God bless his poor soul in the wonderful sky.
Captain Dudley had all the blame,
But to wilfully murder an innocent child,
It was a bloody shame.

Left:
Late Fred Brooks (1940) Poetry to J Jefferies.
Fred Brooks was a likable tough old salt who sailed westward, as second mate, Lulworth, mate of Magdelene, and one season as mate and many more big yachts and racing cutters.

Below:
This photograph taken and allowed by kind permission of Mr Bedford - a retired seafarer and stevedore, and grandson of the late mariner Daniel Parker, first mate on board Meteor.

The Brooks family, Captain Owen Brooks, brother of Ned Brooks, a Mignonette crew member, sailorman Fred Brooks along with his son Archie and grandson David.

Jim Frost of Tollesbury escaped certain death through not sailing on board the yacht.

AMERICA'S CUP 1851
AND IN AMERICA IT STAYED WITH PRIDE FOR 132 YEARS

On the fourth attempt to try and regain the America's Cup to our shores by the World's greatest loser, Sir Thomas Lipton, with the challenge postponed through the outbreak of the 1st World War most of the serving mariners were RNVR and were soon to be fighting for their King and Country, as this story will tell.

Sir William Burton was one of the greatest helmsmen afloat. He was a personal friend of Sir Thomas Lipton, and held the honour of taking the helm at all times on board Shamrock IV in her post world war I challenge for the America's Cup. Being rear commodore of the RHYC 1909-10, vice commodore 1911-35, Commodore 1936-45, he was highly respected by all the Shamrock serving officers and sailors. First rate sailormen of Wivenhoe, Ted, Harry and Bill Hilliard served and sailed on board all the famous yachts. They also sailed about the world as shipmates, yachting with my maritime father: Also serving on board S.Y. Sapphire during the 1930's yachting seasons, and fitting out and sailing out of C & N fine yacht yard Northam, Southampton: Renamed Shamrock Quay, after those five great Shamrocks of fame. Maritime brother, John Hilliard, perished at sea serving on board a merchant ship during the second world war. Upon J.J's recent nautical yarn with Mr. D. Hilliard, it is most rewarding to learn that one the greatest Mastheadsman afloat, and known to J.J during my youth spent on the River Itchen in happy Northam, whilst father was at sea serving on board the magnificent S.Y. Sapphire was none other than 'Monky' Harry Byford, Mr D Hilliard's grandfather. 'Monky' Harry Byford was hero worshipped by our respected sailorman King. Georg.V. and J.J. feel proud of the fact all their treasured memories live on, including my late Uncle Harold Stroud of Whitstable who was indeed, the last first mate to serve on board the R.R.C. Britannia 1931-36.

Shamrock IV was commanded by a famous sailing master, Captain Albert Turner, MVO. The first mate serving Shamrock IV was one of Tollesbury's famous sailing masters, Captain Ned Heard. And the famous helmsman serving on board was Sir William Burton. Some of the mariners in 1914 who sailed across the Atlantic to attempt to regain the Americas Cup to our shores. Serving on board Shamrock IV are eight known sailormen of Tollesbury, as recognised by their relatives and many of the good folk of Tollesbury during my further twenty years of research.

The launching of Shamrock IV at Gosport 1914. On board are A1 sailormen: J. Layzell. D. Heard, R. Heard, L. Heard, R. South, W. Riley, W. Bibby, B. Wilkerson, U. Leavett, C. Wash. B. Heard, W. Cranfield, Rowhedge, William Wadley (nick-name 'Scamp'. B. French, Joe Farthing of West Mersea.

Shamrock IV mooring up, with HMS Victory in the background. May 26 1914.

The crew of Shamrock IV, including Serving Sailormen of Brightlingsea: J. Handley, W. Goff. S. Martin A1 Rigger First Class, G. Taylor, A. Francis. A.. Cox, F. Hempstead, R. Howe, A. Bowles, C. Sharman, William Hazelton, W Dines and William Ryan. Also includes JJ's friend William Fuger of Warsash.

On the outbreak of war in 1914, Sir Thomas Lipton stated yachting would all come back one day, I must add with the greatest respect that many yachting books are indeed of vital records of yachts and American Cup challengers with the history of yachts and their owners. But my lifetime's works, plus a lifetime's collection of maritime recordings, are to remember the gallant masters, navigators, sailmakers and mariners who served on board these gigantic racing machines. The famous yachts could not have been manned without these brilliant sailormen, let alone to become part of our maritime heritage, and in July 1920 the clock had been put back to pre-war summers. Empires had been overthrown, and crowned heads exiled. Casualty lists had darkened every home. In speech after speech, and after every speech an exhausted world had been assured that the old ways had gone forever But here, at Sandy Hook, as a reassurance of continuity, was old Tommy Lipton, with his goatee, his polka dot blue tie, his jaunty tilted yachting cap, looking not one half hour older, challenging again with another Shamrock. The SY Erin, a hospital ship during the War, was sadly lost; the Victoria took her place. In 1914 shipmates on board were sailormen of Bob Howe Snr. and Arthur Bowles, mariners to whom I knew quite well for a nautical yarn, they both lived quite close to my home. Like all mariners, with many a story of the sea to tell, and during the 1st World War, for a while sailorman A1 Robert Howe served on board the luxury yacht of the late Sir Walter Preston, MP. Prior to war and war service during 1st World War, SY Lorna was requisitioned by the Admiralty. A local serving quartermaster named William Thrower, who was serving on board HMS Lorna, a Shamrock sailorman, was ordered by the captain to steer, and to ram a German Submarine off Portland. The crew, sadly, all perished, but one German crew member swam to HMS Lorna and was saved from the sea. He, sadly, died of his injuries upon the deck of the HMS Lorna. This brave sailorman was cared for, and prayers were said during a Christian Burial at sea off Portland.

Sailorman, Arthur Bowles, was indeed very proud of the fact that during the 1st World War he was one of the serving seamen on board the armed passenger liner HMS Carmania, which was engaged in a fierce and bloody sea battle against the German Cruiser, Battleship SS Cap Trafalgar. On January 1st 1915 Arthur Bowles sent a letter to fellow Shamrock IV sailorman, Robert Howe with full details of this battle. A kind member of Mr. Howe's family has given this letter for the JJ Collection.

'SS Carmania was classed as the workhouse and had to often bunker in Lisbon after running at full speed for 24 hours, burning 500 tons of coal per day, whilst chasing the enemy. Arthur Bowles wrote: We are always running at full speed, as we are always chasing some ship. Some of them will not stop when signalled, especially the Dutch Ships, but as soon as we drop a live shell across their bows they damn soon shove her up in the wind. Well, old sport, I had a Christmas card from your cousin Fred Norton. Last time we were in I have a piece of German shell to show you - if I am lucky enough to get over this affair safe, a piece of shell that hit my gun shield and burst and killed my mate, Bussell, a chap belonging to Poole. We had only been in action ten minutes when he got killed, it tore his left side away. It's an awful sight to be in action, no one knows what it is like, only those who have been through it. Our guns on the port side were engaged for the first 50 minutes. Our boats on the port side were blown to pieces, but the signalman sighted a cruiser coming at full speed on the horizon and it proved to be the Dresden so we made off at full speed and double banked her down the stoke holed and the next day the cruiser Bristol came to our assistance and escorted in here where we were eight weeks under repair. We had 293 holes in us altogether, but only 7 under the waterline. Now I haven't the time to write any more, remember me to captain Richers and all the Brightlingsea men on board HMS Lorna and hope we shall all meet again in our little town of Brightlingsea one of these days. With my best to you from your old chum A.J. Bowles PS Should like a line from you any time you care to write, it was a pitiful sight to see him sink and the men swimming in the water, and the sea was the colour of blood all around him. We wanted to lower the few boats we had left to try and save them, but no time. It wasn't a bad scrap for England last hope was it, as we are all reservemen on board'.

On board Sir Thomas Lipton's magnificent SY Erin, 1914, was the late captain Dick Pascoe of Park Road, Cowes, Isle of Wight, being an uncle to a well respected gentleman in the Cinque Port of Brightlingsea, Mr. Harry Nobb, a man of the sea and was sailing at over 90 years of age. My dearest Northam, born and bred, Mother with her Northam sense of humour would always say to Harry 'Be Ye Hampshire Harry to mother?' His reply was 'Be I buggery, I be Isle of Wight Harry'. Being one of not many survivors from the troop ship SS Lankastria, bombed and lost off St. Nazaire, on Sunday 16th June 1940, Harry swam a good half a mile and was picked up by a lifeboat lowered from SS Oransy. Many seafarers and there good, kind families have come into my life including sailormen characters Tom and William Fuger, brothers, of Weatherberth, Warash, Southampton. William served on board Shamrock IV in 1914. Sailorman William Fuger held his Tollesbury shipmates in great esteem along with his brother Tom, who had been a regular crew member and shipmate of my late uncle Albert Jefferies who had served the late gentleman yacht owner Mr. Singer, sewing machine tycoon, for eighteen seasons on board his famous yachts named Xarifa. I much enjoyed my many visits to see these kind folk in their Warsash home.

William Cranfield standing upon the deck being an A1 sailorman and serving 2nd mate. I notice the superb sailorman and rigger, big Alf Dutchy Cranfield, a regular Valkyrie and Shamrocks crew member, and also with a full fifteen years loyal service on board the magnificent 1,250 ton S.Y. Sapphire. Owners, USA Lord and Lady Fairhaven. 'Dutchy' serving as boatswain on board with skipper Edward Pitt of Wivenhoe D.S.M., home Southampton, serving as boatswain's mate, giving fifteen years loyal service. During my own seven years sailing, I served and with Mr. Pitt, 1949-1957 I. was always granted an extra day's leave to make certain that Jeff, as known in yachting circles, would brake my journey home from Southampton. To cross the Rowhedge ferry, run by Ned from the Falkland Islands, to take Big 'Dutchy' a full bottle of regular rum to Rowhedge Cottage. Ned being the last man to run the ferry service and, sadly, died on the ferry boat.

Sailorman, supreme captain, George Block, aged 98 years, was called to higher circles in 1997, who was a respected close neighbour. This gentleman being the son-in-law of sailorman Godfrey, a lifetime sailorman who had served the mammoth Shamrocks Americas Cup Challengers and also steam yacht Vanadis, with members of the Vanderbilt family USA. Skipper George Block was a most remarkable sailorman and navigator and started his sea life at the age of 11 years on board the steam trawler SV General Buller, sailing out of Kesgrave, a vessel which his master mariner father commanded. Mr. Block, who knew and greatly respected my Northam grandparents in Southampton for many years, pre war. Son, Mr, Leslie Block, was a world-travelled deep sea engineer, retired the sea being a most proud gentleman.

In the year 1923 skipper George Block was a serving seaman on board the racing yacht Valdora, under the command of Captain Albert Rowe, winning the King's Cup for their proud owner. Captain Albert Rowe had also served the Royal racing cutter Britannia as first mate, a mariner well worthy of being remembered.

A much respected gentleman known to JJ, holding his Master Mariners qualifications, was Captain Charles Joseph Carter, who mastered a square rig vessel: A1 sailorman, sailing master in sail and steam who, along with Captain Block, was responsible trial masters during the 2nd World War for all vessels built and repaired by Aldous' shipyard, under Admiralty orders, with the good work force and brilliant tradesmen with 750 men, Women and lads clocking in each day, and along with G G Holland, a ships' plumber, and much-respected man, with whom I worked as a small lad. We often ran trials when still working on board, and repairing Admiralty vessels and other craft.

Captain Carter, from his seafaring career, being a respected friend of my maritime father, and shipmate on board SY Sayonara in 1912. A cousin, Mr. Bert Carter, a business gentleman of West Mersea, also knew my grandparents and many of my seafaring relatives in Northam, Southampton from their own seafaring careers. Mr. Bert Carter had served his apprenticeship in the brilliant yacht yard of Camper & Nicholsons, at Northam, Southampton and had sailed as ship's carpenter and as a shipmate, on a few occasions, with my maritime father.

We all had something in common, meaning family connections to the famous yacht Mignonette; a story including murder and cannibalism on the high seas, as captain Carter and Mr. Bert Carter were cousins, blood relatives of captain Dudley.

Captain Charles Joseph Carter was called to higher circles 22nd January 1955 (born 16th March 1876). I shall always remember him as treating all men as fellow human beings, having known hard times at sea whilst serving on board square rig sailing ships. Our masters and mariners are all gone; but certainly not forgotten within JJ's lifetime's maritime recordings.

I would like to pay special tribute to the following: Captain Richard Bond and Captain Mark Norton both of North Devon, who were Master/Owners of coasting vessels, and who also served as navigating officers onboard the world famous Shamrocks.

First rate Warsash sailorman, William Fuger, and his brother William, great friends of JJ, often palled up together for a good nautical yarn at their 'Weather Berth' home, and also, for a tot of rum at the rising sun. For eighteen yachting seasons Tom sailed with my uncle Albert Jefferies on board F.M. Singer's fabulous sail and steam yachts Xarifa N.Y.Y.C.

Skipper Robin Fuger, a most brilliant yacht master who has served the modern-day America's Cup challengers, plus still rigging at the time of writing this book. Fabulous Luxury Racing Yachts Robin being a much respected friend and nephew of Tom and his brother William and for many years now J.J & Robin still exchange our regular phone calls for our nautical yarns to keep in touch.

Tribute to West Mersea yachtsman and fisherman, Mr. Bobby Stoker

On the 26th October 2000 a most sad day occurred to skipper David Stoker, plus all good members of his family, friends and fellow mariners, near and far, young and old. Sailorman supreme, Mr. Robert Stoker, was called to higher circles. He is now in the good Lord's keeping with the rest of our masters and our mariners. I have mostly all their lovely old photographs, and treasure them with affection. St. Peters Church in West Mersea was filled to its fullest capacity with the good folk from far and near to say a final fare-ye-well, and to pay their respects. Colchester Borough Council Leader, Mr. John Jowers, a West Mersea fisherman, made a courageous, emotion-charged tribute to his life long friend, sailorman Robert Stoker.

Stoker's service it was nice to see the late Mr. Fred Good of Harwich, retired skipper owner of trawlers and with RN service 2nd World War, a serving Lieutenant. Fred's father was also a man of sail. Piloting and racing on board all the famous J class racing yachts pre 2nd World War. During Harwich Regattas etc. I also appreciate my kind welcome to the warm and friendly home of Mr. & Mrs. Jim & Lil Clarke. Mrs. Clarke, her maritime family members being the late sailing masters famed for their skills in the art of sail. The Barbrooks of Tollesbury, Mrs. Clarke and fellow members who showed and gave kindness to my friend Ken and I during the fabulous West Mersea regatta are dedicated to the RNLI.

My Endeavour Sailorman friend, Jim Musset, of West Mersea, last, but not least within my story of the sea, late Nancy Musset cared and loved truly her dearest and sweetest father until the very end: I also loved sitting and yarning with this wonderful centenarian, Mr Clary. But one thing that sticks clearly in my mind was when much enjoying his most jovial company, and just prior to God's calling, he looked at me straight in the eyes and said, 'John, I want to ask you a question, do you remember in 1908 when my 18 year old and 14 year old sisters were drowned, with the driver and pony, when crossing the flooded Strood one Sunday morning going to Sunday School?' Of course, JJ was born in 1929, long after this tragedy happened.

I would like to add and pay tribute to my father's friend and shipmate, also serving on board Lulworth in 1926: William De'ath drowned off Zeebrugge, from MY Dahallia, October 28th 1947, under mysterious circumstances.

So here ends my short story, most sacred to all their memory

For those at sea,
The sea is his
O Lord be with us when we sail upon the lonely deep,
Our guard when on the silent deck the midnight watch we keep.
We need not fear though all around mid rising winds we hear
The multitudes of water surge for Thou O God art near.
The calm, the breeze, the gale, the storm that pass from land to land
All, all are thine, are held within the hollow of thy hand.
If duty calls from threatened strife to guard our native shores
And shot and shell are answering first the booming cannons' roar
Be thou the main guard of our host till war and dangers cease,
Defend the right put the sword, and through the world make peace.
To thee the Father three, the Son who earth and sky adore
And spirit, moving o'er the deep, be praise forever more.

Amen.

JJ, retired mariner,
Author, maritime historian.

Crew of Shamrock III. Sir Thomas Lipton in front (centre), on his right (facing), Capt. R. Wringe, on his left, Mr Wm. Fife, designer.

REGISTER OF BRIGHTLINGSEA YACHT MASTERS' CLUB.

Name of Yacht Shamrock I 1901
Owner Sir Thomas Lipton
Captain Robert Wringe.

NAME.	AGE.	CAPACITY.	BELONGING TO.	REMARKS.
Dimble William		1st Mate	Falmouth	very good
Ruffell F.W		2nd "	Blsea	" "
Collier "		1st Stewd	Wivenhoe	" "
Woodward Charles		2nd "	Rowhedge	" "
Taylor Alfred		1st Cook	Blsea	" "
Jefferies Arthur		2nd "	"	" "
Bates Ernest		Carpenter	"	" "
Bragg Walter		Boatswain	"	" "
Byford Alfred		Mst Hd man	Rowhedge	" "
Jose William		Sail Maker	Falmouth	" "
Ruffell Joseph		A.B.	Blsea	" "
Allen Alfred		"	Rowhedge	" "
Everett Burgess		"	Blsea	" "
Nurse Dick		"	"	" "
Wadley "		"	Rowhedge	" "
Goff William		"	Blsea	" "
Francis Joseph		"	"	" "
Aldridge "		"	Rowhedge	" "
Morgan Fred		"	Maldon	" "
Bullen Herbert		"	Rowhedge	" "
Gilders Frank		"	Blsea	" "
Powell John		"	"	" "
Cook James		"	Rowhedge	" "
Pitt Arthur		"	"	" "
Griggs Fred		"	Blsea	" "
Field Hector		"	"	discharged for drunkardness
Rouse Fred		"	"	very good
Brasted Charles		"	"	" "
Bagg Fred		"	"	" "
Lee Harry		"	"	" "
Springett Louis		A.B	Rowhedge	very good
Wisley Harry		"	"	" "
King John		"	"	" "
Musson Charles		"	Blsea	" "
Handley John		"	"	" "
Thrower William		"	"	" "
Wadley Charles		"	Rowhedge	" "
Pittman Charles		"	Tollesbury	" "
W. Barnes Walter		"	Blsea.	" "

REGISTER OF BRIGHTLINGSEA YACHT MASTERS' CLUB.

Name of Yacht Shamrock III
Owner Sir Thomas Lipton
Captain Robert Wringe

NAME.	AGE.	CAPACITY.	BELONGING TO.	REMARKS.
Dimble. W	46	1st Mate	Falmouth	
Ruffell. W	40	2nd "	Blsea	
Woodward. C	29	Chief Steward	Wivenhoe	
Coole R	22	2nd "	" "	
Brown. M.	46	Chief Cook	" "	
Jefferies, A.	28	2nd "	Blsea	
Malcolm. J.	31	Carpenter	Saltcoats Scotland	
Bragg J.	40	Boatswain	Blsea	
Byford W.	38	Masthead Man	Colchester	
Crew W.	30	" "	Falmouth	
Mc. Millan A	29	A.B	Saltcoats Glasgow	
MacKinnon A	36	" "	Sandyford	
Sheddon J	40	"	Saltcoats	
Barnard. A.	26	"	Rowhedge	
Cranfield A.	23	"	" "	
Springett F.	29	"	" "	
Riley M.	24	"	Tollesbury	
Lampson S.	23	"	" "	
Pettican. C	25	"	" "	
Thrower. W.	24	"	Blsea	
Handley J.	30	"	" "	
Linders J.	29	"	" "	
Ham. C.	31	"	Wivenhoe	
Farman. F.	38	"	Gt Yarmouth	
Dowing E.	23	"	[illegible]	
Mc. Keller D.	25	"	[illegible]	
Harvey D.	28	"	Rothesay	
Ward. E	21	"	Tollesbury	
Goff W.	26	"	Blsea	
Angier. F.	22	"	" "	
Gilders F	23	A.B.	Blsea	
Brooks F	26	" "	" "	
Munson. C.	33	" "	" "	
Pitt. C	29	" "	" "	
Wadley A.	33	" "	Wivenhoe	
Martin. S.	27	" "	Blsea	
Vince. A.	30	"	" "	
Pike. W.	30	" "	Wivenhoe	
Day. G	40	"	" Heath	

MARITIME S.Y. ROSABELLE
BY J.J.

The Late Captain Aubrey Goodwin, who was a very close friend
A retired master mariner, but for 42 years at sea he did spend
His good lady wife sailed on board the ship
She loved world travel, she loved every trip
He served the British India Shipping Company for 36 years
Eight of these as mate on the 8,000 ton SS Jalagopal which
Carried Royal Mail and 2,000 passengers.

From Rangoon to Bangladesh was their route
And the Japanese were only four days away on foot
The Captain serving as 1st mate on this 1911 British built ship
Ferried 10,000 civilians to safety on their first trip
They then sailed back and rescued 6,000 more
And by now the Japanese were only two hours away from their doors
Regretfully, they could not go back anymore
As by now the Japanese were breaking down many a front door
The late kind Mrs Goodwin said 'Well Aubrey, our house we could not save
But to rescue all of those people, you and your crew were so brave.

Captain Goodwin stayed at sea
And continued to serve his country
He helped save hundreds of brave masters, officers and crewmembers
From dying in open boats, often only just in time, too
As many a German U-boat crept along the surface, just out of view.

He mastered the 1st BI ship of 16,000 tons in 1968
To boldly enter San Francisco gate
The customs, coastguards and dockers did stare
As one the shore pointed to bow and yelled 'I do declare
There's a swastika up there.'
But that was not the case
As this lucky emblem was no disgrace
For India provided this symbol for everyone to see
And for hundreds of years before the Germans adopted it
It was plain as can be.
The Captain was so proud of Wivenhoe,
The lovely seafaring village where he did dwell
And his master mariner father was born there as well.

For seven years, Captain William Goodwin as 1st mate sailed
The world on his fully-rigged SV Lauraeston
From Liverpool she hailed
About 1901 his wife said, 'Dear William, come home from the sea
And find a nice little job, and be nearer me.'

Captain Arthur Wenlock, OBE, on board SY Rosabelle (Wivenhoe based) was signing on crew
Looked at Captain Williams' master mariner certificate for sail and said 'Yes you'll do!'
For 34 years he did serve as 1st mate
Wherever the owner required his steam yacht, she was always punctual, never late.

A nice home-based job for Captain and crew
For 42 years, the late Mr Brown, as chief steward served her too
Captain A. Wenlock, navigator, was one of the best
And he rectified Admiralty Charts for all of the rest

He marked the charts for all to see
And was highly commended by the Admiralty.

Captain Harvey of Wivenhoe, mastered Rosabelle as well
And being a respected master made the crew happy as well
The SY Rosabelle, in both World Wars did steam
But during the 2nd it was the end of her owner's dream
For off Gibraltar, from the War she did lay
And for some, they thought she was there to stay
But in 1946 a company from the Rock
Took out her plates, numbered them all and placed them in the dock
They were then put on a ship bound for London from there
And then transferred to a ship that was bound for India
A brand new ship for the British India Steam Ship Company was under way
And under her bottom, SY Rosabelle's plates did lay
MV Jalaprhkhsh, of 16,000 tons was her name
And in 1947, Captain Aubrey Goodwin commanded the same
This ship built at Vitapatam contained parts from Rosabelle
And this made the Captain feel very proud as well

Captain Aubrey Goodwin was British through and through
But he was always respected by his loyal Indian officers and crew
He never applied for a medal for all the good work he did do.

In my story I mention all of the sailors, they were such a wonderful breed
And now my main book is published, this story you can read.

Every word of my story is true and I believe in the good Lord above. I have all the good Mariners' household names, nation-wide and photographs. I pray that he will bear witness and bless each and every one with his love. I have tried in my works to pay homage due to all that served our country. I have dedicated the last 40 years of my life to this end.

Wivenhoe is a most important part of maritime history. Captain Aubrey Goodwin, gentleman and lady wife Ann were personal friends of J.J. Mrs Goodwin's gentleman father Mr Russell ran his own business in Rangoon and for part of the 2nd W/W served as Lord Mayor of Rangoon for five terms of office. When Captain Goodwin and his lady wife became wed, The good Indian Boatswain, from on board the ship which Captain Goodwin mastered, made special fancy hand ropes for their bridal carriage, which was pulled by 200 steverdores and records these gospel writings, most sacred to all their memories.

Captain William Goodwin, 1st mate on board S.Y. Rosabelle, circa 1916.

Steam Yacht Rosabelle upon Aldous's slipway in 1926.

Captain Aubrey Goodwin of Wivenhoe, Senior Master of BI Shipping Col, 36 years on board SS Jalagopal.

Rosabelle Crewmembers 1925

Most of whom from Brightlingsea and Wivenhoe.

A. D. Mason
B. B. Blackwood
C. A. Wade
D. J. Richardson
E. E. Lewis
F. G. Smith
G. C. Goodwin
H. W. Eaton
I. J. Marshall
J. T. Moss
K. Lazell
L. T. Gooch
M. T. Percival
N. W. Blyth
W. B. Brown
1st Steward
Y. A. Brown
Z. E. Smith
O. A. Bell
P. P. Goodwin
Q. W. Pitt
R. Captain W. Wenlock
S. Theodore Pimm (Owner)
T. Unknown Crewmember
U. C. Barr
V. G. Drinkwater (Chief Engineer)

Also serving on board, C. Pryke A.B.
1st Mate William Goodwin, Wivenhoe.
2nd Mate Harry Wade, Brightlingsea.
Boatswain Arthur Ellison was killed in Aldous Dock by falling from the Yacht gangway and Mr Ben Finlayson from Scotland took over the Boatswain position on board in 1926.

Steam Yacht Rosabelle. Standing on deck, (rear) Captain William Harvey, (right) First mate Captain William Goodwin, (left) Chief Steward Mr William Brown, all of Wivenhoe.

MARITIME

True stories founded on facts

Sacred Cowes, Isle of Wight, Southampton and Portsmouth, being famous for yachting, and with Camper and Nicholson's being famous for building fabulous yachts. A creation by the human hand, and many designed by Mr. Charles Nicholson, a gentleman who would exchange kind words to us yachtsmen. The working yards had loyal work forces. My late uncle Bert Flood spent fifteen years of his working life with Camper and Nicholson's Northam yacht yard as foreman blacksmith. My late auntie Rose and uncle Bert Flood and six of my cousins were bombed out of their Belvedere Road Club House home during the 2nd World War and it took two whole days to dig them out of their air raid shelter. My late auntie Vera and uncle Charlie Lacy who had 13 children, were also bombed out of their Northam home near Howard's Timber Yard, as it used to be. Quite near the common hard. Camper and Nicholson's, Northam, is now known and respected as Shamrock Quay. My late friend, whom I have known and greatly respected from childhood days, also his kindest lady wife and daughter, Yvonne, and her son. Mr. Durrant served this great yacht yard as foreman rigger for thirty eight years. The previous brilliant foreman rigger, named Mr. Wally Long, father in law of my rigger friend, Mr. Alf Player. Many skills were taught to Mr. Durrant by a supreme rigger by the name of Danny Houston, an Essex man I believe, a friend whom Mr. Durrant hero-worshipped, not forgetting Mr. Durrant's brother Johnny, also a friend.

There was big Ted Crouch of the River Itchen who was a superb bench rigger. Ted had been one of the clan pre 2nd World War, a 40-rater racing skipper who had served with Lord Montague of Beaulieu for many years. Some skippers' names as follows were the admiration of the yachting community. Tommy 'Dutch' Diaper, Topsy Miles, Amyas Leigh. The Rowhedge Cranfields were spoke of and E. Sycamore, R. Wringe, A Turner, C. Carter, Charlie Barr, C. Pallott, A. Hogarth, J. Houston, Parkers. The Diapers and Parkers of the River Itchen, Jack, Bobby, Tug, and Dick. Captains Jim and Jeff Gilby of Bosham. Capt. Randell. Capt'ns Ted and John Banks of The Hythe, Southampton: These were all household names in the yacht racing fraternity. A brilliant river Itchen yachtsman, author J.S, Hughes, had at one time been shipmates with sailorman Robert Hitchens in a ship named SS Dongola. Robert was known as Banjo Bob, and he was at the wheel on board RMS Titanic when serving as one of her quartermasters when striking the iceberg.

During my own yachting career and sailing with late Capt. Edward Pitt D.S.M 2nd World War, of Wivenhoe, we were shipmates for approx. seven years. His Southampton home was 415, Burgess Road, Swaything, Southampton. Mr. Pitt had served as boatswain's mate for fifteen years on board SY Sapphire. His life was saved from drowning by the boatswain, big Alf Cranfield of Rowhedge, whom I would visit leave time at his home. He had also served on board the Valkyries and Shamrocks. Two regular leading firemen, grand kind yachtsman known to myself who served on board SY Sapphire from Wivenhoe, and had made their homes in Southampton in the 1930s, were Moey Carter, and big Jumbo Grenville Smith, being an uncle of gentleman Mr. Woodward of Wivenhoe, and were both still working late in life during the 1950s in Camper and Nicholson's grand yacht yard in happy Northam.

S.Y. SAPPHIRE

Oil tycoons of America, Lord and Lady Fairhaven, who were indeed great benefactors to Great Britain during the 2nd World War, owned SY Sapphire RYS. She carried fifty-eight private crewmembers, the four officers held master mariners qualifications. Mr. Stan Leggerton was chief engineer. Mr. F. Barnard of Rowhedge was 2nd engineer. Mr. and Mrs. Barnard resided in the same house in Southampton for fifty years. She was a most kind lady from Cork and the mother of Professor Brian Barnard of Essex. Mr. Barnard met his future lady wife when she worked in the post office in Cork, she was known to JJ. The late Darky Frank Hedgethorn of Wivenhoe, served as 4th engineer and his late brother Robert served as one of the ship's carpenters.

Mr. Peter Martin, running his own business, Martin Rigging, Lower Swanick, Southampton. I have had the pleasure to know him since he was a lad starting his apprenticeship under Mr. Durrant in the 1950s. We still link up on my Southampton visits. Peter and his team of superb riggers re-rigged J class supreme yacht, Valsheda. She is of splendour and glory and I thank you sir, Captain Simon Bolt (sailing master at the time) for inviting me on board on her completion. It is still a joy and a pleasure for friend Ken Wheeler and I to be greeted at Cowes, Isle of Wight by gentleman, and director of Spencer Rigging, Mr. Harry Spencer, when paying our visits to enjoy a nautical yarn. Always too, a welcome by the famous gentleman photographer Mr. Kenneth Beken, born 1914, and son Keith, born 1951, plus director Mr. Peter Mumford and all members of staff when welcomed, with friendship for a nautical yarn. Mr. Beken RNVR 2nd World War in 1940-1945 commanded an air sea rescue launch, which was built by the famous Aldous Shipyard. He stayed for a time in Brightlingsea with the famous photographer, kind gentleman the late Mr. Douglas Went. My maritime life is all treasured memories, and J.J's best Christmas present, 2006, was, indeed, complimentary letters sent to J.J. by gentlemen Mr Keith Beken and Mr Harry Spencer.

Working in Camper and Nicholsons rigging loft was fabulous Yarmouth man and a friend Mr. Billy Shookford: A most brilliant man at rigging and working aloft. Also Len Diaper of the River ltchen. Len was also a shipmate of my father, a superb yachtsman, rigger and true friend. The Diapers, Parkers, Mathews, Candys, Bradens, Cozens, Capt. Len Evans and his brother Tom, who was a chief steward, were all famed and household names along the River ltchen. Tough sailorman Bill Braden I had known all my life. He had been shipmates with my maritime father, sailing the world on board SY Tuscarora after the 1st World War. He was a shipmate on board Lulworth in 1926, and during the 1930s on board SY Sapphire NYYC, when Lord and Lady Fairhaven loaned the yacht to Sir Winston Churchill for a good will visit to sail out East. During 1951, on board MY Virginia RYS, was the Duke and Duchess of Westminster, who chartered the yacht to cruise inside the Artic Circle. Sailorman friend, Bill Braden, as tough as old leather, age seventy years, was, indeed, one of our serving crewmembers.

Last, but not least in my story, yachtsman late Don Mills. Don and I were pals from my youth and grew up together in Northam. Don and his yachtsman brothers, John and David, their mother was so kind, a Northam lady and a true friend of my mother and family, Mrs. Mills, also schooled in Northam. In 1912 when 140 Northam school pals had lost a relative overnight on board Titanic: With due respects, the riggers were removing a Trinity House Light Vessel 3/4 ton mast when, just by sheer accident, the paul on the cog wheel accidentally slipped, and the handle sprang back, taking Don's young life at 40 years. The yard closed for the day out of respect. God bless their memory one and all. 1948, Port Isaac skipper, shipmate and friend, Jim Cann: Sent to me his very last Christmas card in 1985. Jim started sea life on board trawlers. He served on board Endeavour in 1934 and 1937, RN 2nd World War on board minesweepers. Jim and his kind lady wife, Blanche, were great friends. Supreme sailorman Jim was called to higher circles at a Fawley, Southampton dinner and dance evening 1985, aged 77 years.

My lifetime's recordings are most sacred to all their memory.

J.J's maritime friend, Roy Griggs, world travelled sailorman, RNVR. During his time at sea in the 1st World War, his treasured son Derek, aged seven years, was tragically killed by a naval lorry near the local cinema, which is now the doctors' surgery. Sadly, the naval ship Mr. Griggs was serving on board was due to sail out of Portsmouth and, sadly, he was not permitted compassionate leave.

During the early 1950s, Roy Griggs skippered the sea going Motor yacht Seawitch, which was owned by Maxwell Reid and the fabulous actress Joan Collins, from the days when they spent much time in Brightlingsea.

Back to Aldous shipyard. During the 2nd World War years with the two shipyards, Aldous, and James, along with the river Colne and Wivenhoe and Rowhedge shipyards, there are many stories of the sea still to be told. The hardy fishermen, RNVR, from all the seaports of Great Britain made up the many crewmembers who so bravely served on board these converted trawlers and drifters. Where the workmanship on board many of these vessels was carried out in Aldous' shipyard and Wivenhoe to convert these craft for minesweeping: Helping to safeguard fellow mariners in peril on the sea. Many a brave sailorman lost their own lives sailing out from Brightlingsea and Harwich and further afield. As a lad, aged thirteen, during the first year of the 2nd World War I often spent the day afloat with my father and the crew on board steam tug Bricklesea, tending many of the ships laying in the Colne and Blackwater. The tug was also waterboat for all ships under the Admiralty.

I can recall some of the ships by name, being serviced by Aldous shipyard and sailing out of the river Colne; some never to return, with much loss of human life, and their ships were their mariners' graves. Some bodies of sailormen were recovered and were laid to rest in our local cemetery at All Saints Church, Brightlingsea. Ruddocks' premises, High Street, was the mortuary. Names of ships: John and Alfred, Sturnes, Strive, Three Kings, Internos, Jennie Leash, Rosedale (lost) Drummond (lost). THV Strathern, lost off Clacton, 16 crew perished. One of the Grimsby trawlers converted for minesweeping and based in the river Colne was ST Staunton, her registration number was GY350 and her name remained with the same owners for thirty-three years. The 1st mate and two of her gallant crew members, had been invited by my maritime father to a Sunday lunch at my parents' rented old cosy cottage at no. 11, Nelson Street, Brightlingsea. Ten shillings per week had to be paid to our kind old red-faced gent, landlord Mr. Ernest Field. He was a shipwright who had served and sailed on board Valkyries and Shamrocks as one of the ship's carpenters, with his close friend Mr. George Day of Wivenhoe. My mother had sailed the seas as a laundry girl on board liners, world cruising. She married my maritime father on 8th October 1928. Being a most kind lady, on the Sunday prior to 28th July 1940 she had cooked a grand lunch for father's invited fellow seafaring friends. One being the mate from on board HMS Staunton, and two jovial sailors, I believe from on board the Staunton. One by name, Jimmy Edwards, probably as I recall from North Shields as his young wife had come to Brightlingsea to spend a couple of days with her pleasant husband. These jovial mariners said their last farewells during the evening to return to HMS Staunton. The ship left the river Colne that same evening I believe on the low water to sweep the Thames estuary and out through the Burrow Deeps. Just below the river Colne, near the Knoll Buoy, this grand old ship that had faced the elements of the sea and storms, protecting her gallant crew, fishermen of England, for thirty three years, on 28th July 1940 sadly struck a magnetic mine. That same selfish sea of which man often reaps a good harvest of fish, the cruel sea, once more had sadly and most tragically taken another harvest of brave mariners in return. I pray to god this information and true story is beneficial to a gentleman from Grimsby, Mr. James Freer, grandson of the serving mate on board HMS Staunton. He wrote recently, a cry for help, probably hoping against hope, after so many years of ever finding any person knowing of this ship; yet alone knowing of his gallant maritime grandfather and crewmembers. Most sadly, from mother's old rented cottage, many of us heard the explosion when the two ships were lost. When my maritime father came home the following day from on board steam tug Bricklesea I can still picture my mother crying on hearing that sad news.

Another sad day during the war years, the mine sweeper Jennie Leash was being prepared for mine sweeping and upon a very dark, cloudy day with low cloud and drizzly rain one Saturday afternoon, I was about to return indoors from down our garden, (outside wc), when roaring overhead were these two German Dornia bombers which had just dropped their bombs and were heading back for Germany. This was indeed another sad day for our small community at the time. One of the bombs had dropped at the stern of the tug Bricklesea upon part of the Jefferies family oyster layings. Father lay upon the deck of the tug and was covered from head to toe in mud. The old SV Bricklesea saved his life. His old cycle, which a grand man, Mr. Norton Cox, had rebuilt for father, the saddle was blown clean off the bike. Mother, with her Northam sense of humour, said to Dad 'It was a good job you were not sitting upon it then!' Little did she know. Father and his friends, Jeff Dines Snr shipmate, and big George Rickwood, who was with dad racing on board the 24 metre Lulworth 1926, he was a hard case and served as number two Mastheadsman on board. Sadly, one of the bombs had dropped between the dock and the bow of Jennie Leash and blown to pieces Mr. Robinson of 24, Hurst Green, local, and a young naval rating who arrived by train and had just got below into the foc'sle to unpack his kit bag. Dad and his friends had been to hell and back during the 1st World War and faced death. They volunteered for the ghastly task of recovering the parts of their bodies. Mother did not know of this at the time in question. A son of Mr. Robinson, David, he and I worked together in Aldous shipyard for three years during the war, with many sad stories to tell of the coming and going of the ships. David's mother was a kind lady, and his sister Margaret was a fabulous singer. Mr. Tommy Wright and Mr. Harold Groves were friends of my maritime father, and they often went out to the river Colne to work on board the ships, after serving their engineers apprenticeship in Aldous shipyard.

Mr. Billy Ruffell RN, 2nd World War, Mr. Len Rowley RN Submariner, Mr. Basil Grimsby MN, Mr Harold Graves RN, Mr. Tommy Wright Royal Fleet Auxiliary and MN. After the first year of war these men took an active part in war and Mr. Tommy Wright, world travelled, Chief Engineer, retired, is indeed a friend and one of my own shipmates from when I served as a seaman AB on board passenger ships the Amsterdam and the Arnham, sailing out of Harwich. between my yachting career. I must add Captain Harry Keeble, a world travelled master mariner who was greatly respected by fellow men. He was indeed one of the kindest gentlemen masters I had the honour to sail with. He is well known and respected as Big H.

Just after the tragic loss of HMS Staunton, the HMS Drummer was soon to follow, with the sad loss of many of her crewmembers, and many who were injured. Mr. Harold Groves, just prior to serving in the RN, was still working on board as the Drummond was leaving the river Colne just as the Grace Darling, one of the three liberty boats, was at the mouth of the creek. Crewed by Bill Hazleton Snr, a Shamrock IV sailorman and 'Oakum' Pammet, sailorman, who had served and raced on board many famous yachts. The three liberty boats, Nemo II, Gazelle, and Grace Darling, had three local sailormen as serving crewmembers in each boat, with a relief crew included. As a lad, I knew them all. Their rest hut, with bogey stove, was made up from part of the hard shelter, and Mr. Albert Potter was in charge. This man, being one of our naval cadet instructors when thirty-eight of us local lads were trained with 303 Lee Enfield rifles, and taking them home with live ammo. This caused much friction with the local home guard, who only trained with broom poles. They did stints of sea defence duty to stop the Germans from landing. However, Mr. Harold Groves very often would say how lucky he was that the crew on board MV Gazelle, went alongside HMS Drummer and picked him up; this being his lucky day. There is indeed always the humorous side of being afloat, so to speak. Mr. Johnny Shields was one of the RNVR fishermen who had served on board HMS Internos during the 2nd World War. One Saturday afternoon whilst on watch on board he told my maritime father to go on board the Internos and tend to the rum jug. If there was one thing my father enjoyed better than a tot of rum, was another tot to follow. Johnny said that he would tend to the water. Well, after a good look round on board, father could not be found by either Johnny nor the crew or skipper, Noble Field, Jeff Dines Snr and engineer Billy Bird. Jeff Dines with his quiet ways and dry sense of humour said 'Christ, I hope our pal Arthur hasn't fallen overboard and made a hole in the water.' They had not looked down the foc'sle on board the tug when, suddenly, Johnny smelt smoke. He shot down the foc'sle of the tug and up again to fetch a bucket full of water. Dad had fallen asleep by the foc'sle stove and is stern end of his boilersuit was well alight. Johnny doused my father with the bucket of water. My father-in-law, William Walker, was a regular soldier 2nd Battalion Suffolk Regiment. POW three and a half years, Burma Railroad. At the end of hostilities was a neighbour of Johnny and his pleasant lady wife Dolly, they showed great kindness. After one week in a military hospital he had to make his own way home, no help in those days. Reg Briggs and Joe Smith, driver and Conductor on Eastern National bus showed great kindness and help, but sadly in those days Samaritans for all our forgotten war heroes were few and far between. On the third week home he was told you are used to hard work after working for the Japanese 25 hours a day, 8 days a week. As a seven stone man, reduced from fourteen stone, he was offered a job on the refuse cart - needless to say no more! However. Mrs Shields most quietly and discreetly held her own feelings for the mariners from losing their lives at sea. This lady still places flowers upon the graves of mariner friends of hers and husband Johnny. They are all gone but will never be forgotten and my lifetime's dedication and works remain most sacred to all their memory. For all good folk with feelings towards our heritage, a point of river Colne interest: We do have our own RAF Spitfire still buried in Brightlingsea side of the river Colne. Our local river police, who carried a Bren gun on board the police boat Vigilant, shot this down in error. The river police were disbanded soon after. This was during the first dog-fight over Essex. My friend David Gant and I saw this Spitfire nosedive in smoke into the mud. The lucky pilot did bail out and was just soaked and, luckily, was not injured. He was swearing well on the old original causeway. The Spitfire is between mud and clay and could still be well preserved and I do know its location.

Having myself boarded the Grimsby steam trawler, Staunton, in early July 1940 during my summer holiday as a lad, whilst the old steam tug Bricklesea tended all ships laying at anchor in the river Colne and Blackwater. It was indeed a heart breaking time for many good folk in our small Cinque Port town of Brightlingsea when we all learnt of the sad news, prior to the announcement by the Admiralty that the former Grimsby trawler Staunton, skippered by a master of the sea, S.W. Campbell RNR, was tragically lost off the Knoll Buoy: This being not too far away from our local estuary. It was a grand old ship and a brave sailorman's grave for all her gallant crewmembers, of whom some I had the joy to meet and talk to. After the 2nd World War had gladly ended I myself worked for a time on board the old smack CK Sunbeam with a character skipper, of late, named Basil Steady. We often towed his 30ft. long beam trawl around HMS Staunton when the skate were plentiful. Approximately five fathoms deep, at low water, one could see the black shadow, and reflection during sunlight, upon the sea from her black painted hull. Having seen, and knowing some of her gallant crew members in life, it was very heartbreaking to know that this ship must be their grave, as no bodies were ever recovered from Staunton. It is a known fact that the few mariners who continued to fish during the 2nd World War fetched many dead sailormen and airmen into Harwich and Brightlingsea. Myself and my naval cadet pals, late Harry Moss, Harry Ainger, David Gant and Peter Revett RN, had all seen many of these brave ones lined up on the old original wooden causeway, waiting for the RAF or RN lorries to take these poor souls to the building which had become known as the local mortuary - Ruddocks, the electricians. The ladies who drove these lorries with fellow WRENS and, WRAFS were very brave and courageous. The dead British and German alike, all were being some mothers' sons, and Mr Reg Griggs, a staunch Christian and undertaker respectfully cared for them all.

CREW MEMBERS

HMS Staunton carried eighteen crewmembers of which thirteen hardy fishermen RNR made up the gallant crew, all from Grimsby. Captain S. Campbell was her proud skipper, aged 35 years, of 40, Humberstone Road, Grimsby. He and his lady wife had 4 sons. Sidney, his father's namesake, aged ten; Walter was only five and a half; Alan aged 4 and Malcolm aged two and a half. Captain Campbell had been at sea, starting at the age of 14 years and for a man of his young age he had been master for almost seven years.

The 1st mate serving was James E Freer who had two children. A boy aged six and a girl of eighteen months. His own father had been lost at sea after the 1st World War. They lived at 101, Patrick Street, Grimsby. 3rd Mate was Frederick Horace Bye, aged 42, of 45, Hilyard Street. He left a wife and three children. Chief Engineer, George Lovell Garner, aged 59, of 62, Combe Street, Cleethorpes. He had served 1st World War at sea. 2nd Engineer was Fred Cass, aged 42, of 42, Albert Street, Grimsby. AB Edward William Pennock, aged 49, of 66, King Edward Street, Grimsby; a veteran of the 1st World War with thirty three years at sea. AB William Donaldson, aged 50, of 149, Hewhaven Terrace, Grimsby. AB Frank Horsley aged 33, of 63, Albion Street, Grimsby. AB Joseph Alfred Robinson aged 36, of 216, King Edward Street. Trimmer Cyril Howden aged 34, with four children of 19, Eastgate Terrace, Grimsby. He held a premonition that he would lose his life at sea. Trimmer Thomas Wilson aged 37, of 89, Eleanor Street, Grimsby. Trimmer Alfred Horace Lingard aged 40 of 125, Harold Street, Grimsby. He had a wife and three children. All were married seafarers except Wilson. The Staunton owners were Standard Steam Fishing Company of Grimsby

The HMS Drummer took over the same area at sea for mine sweeping at low water and sadly came to grief eight days after the loss of Staunton. She suffered the same fate a few yards East of Staunton's grave. Us natives of Brightlingsea sadly heard once more the explosion caused by a magnetic mine. Four of her crewmembers were killed and the survivors were landed at Brightlingsea after being saved by patrol Yachts. Under the Admiralty, the little ships were painted grey and it saddens myself, as a retired seafaring man, author and maritime historian, when reading over the years the inaccurate reports from hearsay, of survivors only being offered tea at the Anchor Hotel. This sad report is very much inaccurate. Hot rum was always freely given by Mrs Gould and her sister, Mrs Fisher. Yes, my kind readers, I myself saw the arrival of survivors, many a brave sailorman and airmen, British and German alike, during my naval cadet days. With fellow school pals, as previously mentioned, together with my late brother Alfred, the late Lewis Branch, all of us being naval cadets. We all witnessed the kindness towards fellow mariners given by the proprietors of the fabulous riverside Anchor Hotel. The late Mr. and Mrs. Cliff, and Elsie Gould and members of her family, all of which are remembered and respected for their kindness to those in peril on the sea. They most certainly helped by taking towels and blankets down the old wooden causeway to comfort many that were wet, cold and wounded. Harry Ainger often talks to me of how one German airman, saved from the sea, spat upon everyone trying to comfort him. I pray to God my words are of comfort to many of the relatives at Grimsby and indeed, further afield, who lost their loved ones at sea and in the air. Gentleman, Mr. Percival, built the Anchor Hotel in 1903. He was the father of Mrs. Elsie Gould and Mrs. Tots Fisher. Mr. Cliff Gould, respected husband of Elsie, was a man of the sea with thirty-eight years to his credit. The son of a famous yacht master. he served the Liverpool Salvage Company for thirty-eight years and was much involved on board the salvage ship SS Ranger, which was much involved with HMS Thetis, a 2nd World War submarine tragedy: But that is another story.

The Anchor, Brightlingsea, was indeed headquarters for the Admiralty, with Commander Campbell in command, and he was greatly respected by all. Captain Arthur Aldridge, a most kind man and a family friend. He was head of salvage operations to the local East Coast. During the 1st World Ward Mr. Aldridge was awarded a medal for bravery, being a crewmember on board a Q ship. The crew were all disguised as fishermen. The ship, holding a record for sinking German ships, they were not permitted to pick up survivors, neither to take any prisoners. Mr. Aldridge had also served as a crewmember on board the famous Shamrocks, 1901/2. As seaman and during the 2nd World War he piloted an MTB out of Brightlingsea on a secret mission across the Channel. Arthur Aldridge Jnr, a family friend had hidden up on board this MTB when his father thought that Arthur had been sent ashore. This was not the case. Arthur, as a lad, was still on board the MTB during her secret mission. Many of us lads were allowed on board many ships, being young naval cadets looking after dinghies and tenders for the liberty boats. We were known and respected by the serving crewmembers.

During the start of the war I enjoyed my jovial days afloat, fishing on board CK Wonder with skipper owner Alfred Carter, and son, Michael. Mr. Carter being a brother of the famous John Carter of RRC Britannia fame. The wonder had to lie up for duration of war, but many happy days were spent on board and also after the war.

Magnetic mines had brought bad luck to the newly founded base at Brightlingsea. The NOIC, Captain Henniker-Heaton, reported to the FOIC at Harwich as follows:

"I regret to have to report the loss of HM Trawler Staunton on the night of 26/27th July in the following circumstances: - HM Staunton left her anchorage off Brightlingsea at 1800 on 26th and proceeded to her patrol between Wallet Spitway Buoy and North Buxey Buoy. She was last sighted by MY Sarawara at 2200 steaming on this patrol. She failed to return on the following day, 27th inst. And all skippers of trawlers and drifters in her vicinity were questioned as to whether they had sighted her or heard any explosion in the area, and it was ascertained that no explosion had been heard

The MY Giroflee was cruising as examination vessel two miles from Staunton's patrol during the whole of the 2th, and reported that nothing was to be seen of her. All trawlers, drifters and motor patrol boats were ordered to keep a special lookout for her when they again proceeded to sea at 1800. I proceeded out in MY Giroflee to search for her on the morning of the 28th, and at 1130 in dead low water sighted the tops of two masts showing 4ft above the water, south fifty degrees east, 8 cables from Knoll buoy. I sent a boat to investigate, and they reported that they were trawler masts-the foremast being still firm in the ship, and the aftermast having broken away - they brought this spar back with them. I buoyed the position and reported this on my return to harbour. During the night of 26/27th there were several severe lightning and thunderstorms, accompanied by torrential rain, and great enemy air activity, and it appears that these circumstances may be the cause of no explosion having been heard in Staunton's vicinity.

I regret to come to the conclusion that HM Trawler Staunton was blown up by enemy mine, and that there are no survivors. Deck Hand Clarke of Staunton had been given special leave and was not on board on the night of 26/27th.

Sailorman Hazel White, who was in command on board HMS Triton, under the Admiralty, playing an active role for the Admiralty was in the vicinity at the time of the loss of Staunton. Mr. White was also a family friend of my maritime father, and also a close friend of my late Uncle Harold Stroud RNVR, 2nd World War, who was the 1st mate on board the RRC Britannia 1931/36. Mr. White was a brilliant Mastheadsman and a most agile man. He had raced on board the fabulous J Class Cambria. He would also visit my Northam, Southampton grandparents pre 2nd World War during his yachting career. He knew the crew on board Staunton and Drummer. We often quietly discussed them. Mr. White was later in life the proprietor of one of the two pubs at Heybridge Basin, The Ship: The other being the Jolly Sailor.

MY Giroflee in 1962, our kind owner was Mr. Mackay RTYC. Our good engineer and friend was Mr. Dick Farrow of St. Ives, Cornwall. He was a nephew of the only survivor from the St. Ives Lifeboat tragedy, and in the late 1940s Dick was a serving engineer on board schooner Zaka, owned by the late actor Errol Flynn, who was a very kind yacht owner to his crew; with a British captain and a good and kind friendly West Indian crew. Being good company on runs ashore when we linked up in the Mediterranean.

The River Colne holds many secrets and stories of the sea. My friend, the late Billy Neill, was the serving mechanic on board the Clacton-on-Sea lifeboat for 30 years. He was also chief engineer on board MY Giroflee HMS under the Admiralty, 2nd World War. The three local liberty boats, Gazelle, Grace Darling and Nemo II were the Clacton pleasure beach boats owned by the late Mr. Newt King, Albert Potter, Reg Lawes and other shareholders. These were requisitioned for the duration of war.

Nemo II. For many years after hostilities, my friend Mr. Richard Harman ex RN 2nd World War, retired coxswain of the Clacton lifeboat, and I spent many happy hours running passengers. Dick's Brightlingsea members of mariners, the Barbers, with their own fishing vessels, of which half the family were drowned and the other half starved trying to earn their livelihood. It was a joy to know and to socialise after the 2nd World War with the Clacton-on-Sea Lifeboat crewmembers. They tried so desperately hard to save the life of Flight Officer Raymond King, a brave pilot who sadly died of hypothermia.

IN MEMORIAM

Flight Officer Raymond King.
436th Fighter Squadron US 8th Air Force.
Crashed off Clacton
13th January 1945.
Proudly remembered by relatives
Alvin and Jane Stuard (USA)
and East Essex Aviation Society.

Another sad story of the river Colne: During the 2nd World War a Stirling bomber flew back to England from her mission, 70 miles off course. Sadly she was shot down, in grave error between Point Clear Bay and the 2nd Beach, by our own Ack Ack gun fire. It was a most tragic affair. Being half ebb tide those who might have survived were trapped inside and drowned. Had it have been low water they might have stood a chance. The RAF cleared all the wreckage in 1953. During my leave from on board MY Virginia RYS, thirty two private crewmembers, the RAF lads asked me what my interest was with the Stirling. So I most politely told them this story.

My school pal, Jimmy Durrant, and I played hooky from school to pay a visit across the creek from Brightlingsea to St. Osyth Stone. The navy lads obliged us both with a lift. On return we ducked down in the bottom of the landing craft in order not to be seen from HMS Nemo. On our return to school the following day some kind creep had reported us to our Headmaster, the cane being Mr. Palmer's best friend. Our hardearned history lesson had cost Jimmy and I four of the best upon each hand. Two of the wheals on my left hand were broken open. He did enjoy this, but we did not! Jimmy and I both had our heads down the loo for an hour or so calling out for hoo-ey, sick and bad.

Sailorman Mr. George Bragg, who is mentioned in my story, during the 2nd World War he tended the ships with stores with the late Mr. Berkie Woolvett, who was also a freeman of the river Colne, the same as Mr. Bragg. Mr. Bragg almost made ninety years in age. As a lad I worked with these jovial men. Mr. Woolvett owned the lovely little motor skiff CK United. I often fished in the Colne on board during the war and after, out with Mr. Woolvett, a man who never wore sea boots. He wore only plimsolls and no socks! Winter and summer alike, a hard man. Three of the Stirling bomber crewmembers somehow escaped from the aeroplane from under a few feet of water above the wreckage, but sadly they perished, being severely wounded. One poor soul with his legs almost shot away was picked up in the River Colne along with two fellow dead airmen. This was by Mr. Bragg and Mr. Woolvett in the CK United. The brave airman with his legs shot away, in death, was still clutching hold of his birthday card sent to him by his wife on the previous day.

TRIBUTE

Sailorman, Mr. George Bragg, local, often talked to me when I worked alongside him on the River Colne as a youngster. He told me of the SY Sapphire upon which he proudly served: This vessel, owned by the Duke of Bedford, being named the Goissa for war service. Mr. Bragg had enjoyed yachting at its best and at its worst. During the 1st World War as a young seaman, whilst serving on board the SY Sapphire, the vessel was requisitioned by the Admiralty and served in the Dardenelles. At the entrance to a place named Shannack, the SY Sapphire struck 2 mines and sadly was out of sight within ten minutes with the loss of eighty nine lives, officers and ratings. Mr. Bragg was at the stern end when this grand lady slid beneath the waves, sinking stern first. The only thing Mr. Bragg thought of doing, and of course wearing no life jacket, he ran for'd and was on the stem head when the vessel went down and as she sank Mr. Bragg went down with her. He thought 'Oh my God' and prayed for all his life was worth. God must have been kind and answered his prayers as he came up again, and managed to catch hold of a floating hatch board. Mr. Bragg had two daughters, one residing at Tollesbury, one in Brightlingsea and two seafaring sons, John and Tony. John had sailed with me on board MY Virginia in 1952, med cruising. Tony, being a deep sea engineer, for many years sailing on tankers and containerships, travelling all over the world. Tony enjoyed trawling with his nice little craft on the River Colne, for fish - and why not? As, like myself, this is his birthright. At the time of writing he is still our local hard master. Mr. Bragg also had two seafaring brothers. Captain William Bragg being. of pleasant nature, who served at sea during the 1st World War with his good yachting friend and school chum, the late Robert Howe Jnr. local, being a man who had proudly served the J Class and the Shamrocks. Mr. Bragg served for many years as master of Everards Coasting firm until his retirement. His other brother was Reg Bragg. He was aged 25 when lost from HM Patrol Yacht Verona off Cromarty. Other members lost in this tragedy were George Salmon aged 46, a local yachtsman, William J. Steady aged 47, Harry T. Doyle Sub. Lt. RNR aged 33. The ship was lost off Cromarty on February 24th 1917. Mr. Doyle's body was recovered and laid to rest in Brightlingsea Mariners Church Yard.

My mother made great friends with the late Annie Peirson, a very kindly lady who lived close by. One day, in 1956, Mr. George Bragg passed this grand lady in our local High Street and said 'Hello Annie', Annie said 'Hello George' as though it were only a week in not seeing each other. In fact many years had drifted by. During the 1st World War Mr. Bragg was billeted at North Shields, Annie's old hometown, with her kind mother. The name Annie Peirson is not well known in Brightlingsea but she took her place proudly at Australia House, London for the Armistice Service every year as an honoured guest. Annie's brother was none other than Jack Simpson, with the donkey, who so gallantly fetched many a wounded soldier during the 1st World War down to safety from the hills in the Dardenelles. He was killed doing the job. He was made a hero by the good Australian people and was put on their postage stamps to prove it. It was not much recognised by people in this country as he had jumped ship in Australia, and on the outbreak of the 1st World War he joined the Army and went to fight with the good Australian fighting forces and became their hero.

As I sit here writing my memoirs my own heart reaches out towards all the family members, friends and community of the sad loss, 12th January 2000, of the 21 metre fishing vessel and her seven gallant crewmembers of the scallop dredger Solway

Harvester, caught in a fierce storm off the Isle of Man. Her gallant crewmembers all lived in the nearby village of Isle of Whithorn. God bless all men who go down to the sea in ships. This has devastated the whole community.

All I have written about are mostly gone, but they will never be forgotten. My greatest prayer for the years 2006 and onwards is that my own lifetime's maritime recordings shall be vital and appreciated throughout the world. For all good seafaring folk and people who respect our maritime heritage. I also pray that the light of the Lord shall shine brighter for the world with the years ahead.

Sailorman Albert Rose proudly showing his catch of sprats. Albert served as a seaman on board the famous Shamrocks, and for many winters he Skippered down channel escollopping.

Crew of the famous White Heather, 1906. With all serving Brightlingsea crew-members. The Master, Capt'n George King, (holding the wheel). To his left, William Aldous the Brilliant serving First Mate. Front row far right, Bob (Totty) Francis.

MARITIME
More stories

A much-respected River Itchen mariner, and a shipmate of JJ, Bill Braden, was due to sail as 2nd mate with Captain Tom Diaper, and the maritime Candy families were household names along the River ltchen. Alf Candy had sailed on board the famous Shamrocks and had sailed with the famous Captain Sycamore, and his maritime father supplied fish to the crew on board the Shamrocks, of which he had caught with his River ltchen sailing smack: It was my pleasure to know such a gentleman and a mariner, R.N. 2nd World War, who resided near Peartree Church, the resting place of many a mariner. Regretfully, sailorman Alf Candy drowned accidentally from a boating accident in the Solent River. Gone but not forgotten. During the 1927-1928 yachting seasons Dad was honoured to be serving on board Sir John and Lady Thornycroft's dutch barge yacht, Joyeen R.Y.S.

Gentleman yacht owner, R.A. Sir Richard Fairey of Fairey Marine, was a great aviator pioneer and kindly offered to fly dad and the crew of the Joyeen home from Southampton to the river Colne, in turn that he might pick up some of our native oysters. The crew of the Joyeen had one and all sailed the world under canvas, but they all declined the kind offer by saying' No Sir, you will not get us up in one of those new damn fangled things!'

Well, as stated within my recordings the 2nd World War had, most sadly, started when dad was quite content and happy to be one of the crew members serving on board the magnificent schooner yacht Lelanta owned by a resident of Warsash, gentleman All Gardiner, a director of Yardley Cosmetics. He was a most considerate and kind owner and, as a family, my late brother Alfred and I would often have a few days and nights on board Lelanta laying at the river Hamble. The yacht had to be hurriedly laid up at Lukes Yard, Hamble, on the outbreak of war. We had to say our farewells to our many Northam relatives and friends.

Uncle Jack Beadle, having two wealthy grandfathers, James Smith, bargee, warehouse owner apprentice to Mr. Tate on the river Thames. Being an apprentice on board the British barquentine Galena, owned by Samuel Shutes of Liverpool. This fine ship foundered near Haystack Rock, Oregon U.S.A. on November 13th 1906, and for three years my uncle recorded every day of his working life on board ship. He recorded for eight years with the early settlers of Oregon: Wests, Bradens, Adairs, Wilkinsons and Smiths, some who left Glossop in England to travel overland by prairie schooner. On the outbreak of the 1st World War my uncle returned to England the same day as my maritime father and his shipmates from serving on board the steam yacht, Warrior, with the famous members of the Vanderbilts family. Dad, returning home from America to fight for his country, left New York on the first day of the war on board S.S. Olympic. My maritime father first met Jack Beadle Jnr. after the 1st World War when his grandfather, on his father's side of the family, was Charles Hyde Beadle of Woodhall Estate, Newport, Essex. This gentleman purchased for his grandson the lovely sailing barge Lord Kitchener, built by Foster of Emsworth at the turn of the century. There was not a tighter boat and she hardly took in any water or rain during her four years whilst on a mooring marking a wreck at the East End of the Isle of Wight.

This vessel, during the Royal Yacht Squadron regattas at Cowes, sacred Cowes, the home of famous yachting for fourteen years in succession was a mark boat, and a very sad day for J.J. and all family members when my uncle Horace Parker, from the river Itchen, Mate on board SB Lord Kitchener for eleven years, was injured on board in 1937 and died the following day. Jack Beadle served on board the British 3,000 ton barquentine Galena which foundered on the Oregon Coast, Clatsop County USA, on the 13th November 1906. Being a bound apprentice, together with his best friend, Billy Marshall, also an apprentice, should have returned to their Shipping Company but failed to do so, whereby the owner of the Galena, Mr. Samuel Shutes, sailed from Liverpool in search of them, but with a 500 dollar bounty on their young heads they went into hiding in the mountains, hunting for food with a rifle: Sometimes food was left for them by settler friends. (This is all part of my family tree, and quite unique, covered by a wealth of chronicles, log books and photographs). Jack recorded: 'These are wonderful people. No-one gave the show away during the two weeks hunt. The all clear was given when Mr. Shutes left for England. Mrs. Dawson of Oregon had a heart made of pure gold.

At the outbreak of the 1st World War Jack Beadle returned to England to fight for his country, but it broke his heart to leave loved ones and the many friends who had been so kind to him, and the crew of the Galena. They were overwhelmed by kindness and hospitality given to them by Mr. and Mrs. Josiah West, Alf Dawson, and the Wilkinson family, where they stayed and worked for these good people for eight years. Billy Marshall, mentioned above, later passed his Masters' qualifications on board HMS Conway. He also passed his Masters' qualifications on American ships in America.

During the Great War, Jack Beadle palled up with nine American Snipers, fighting fierce and bloody battles for liberty and freedom, during the Dardenelles Campaign in 1915. The brave heroes of Texas were as follows: Sergeant House, received DSM and was highly recommended for a VC, being a brave hero, (this recommendation was never forwarded owing to the sad fact that Company Officer Major Younghusband, Mr. Bolton, and Mr Browning were killed the following day April 1916), Texan brothers Bill and Firl Craze, brothers Norton and Firl Crockett (believed to be relatives of Davy Crockett), Sergeant Bill Rucker, Sergeant Bill Bailey, Sergeant Cory, Sniper Bill Smith, and Sergeant G.W. Covington.

Sunday 23rd April 1916 - poor old Rucker got one through the head. Rucker was living when last I heard of him when he got to the field ambulance. I cried like a kid when he got hit. Galena apprentices from Cowes, Isle of Wight, Victor Cook and Angus Brown were both sons of sea captains. Victor Cook was killed from aloft. Uncle recorded when his Texan friend in battle, Sargeant Sniper Rucker, was hit in the head and was carried to the ambulance. My uncle recorded 'I cried like a kid'. Uncle never did know if he made it or not, I pray to God that I may find out some day. My uncle's lifetimes chronicles, log books, Lloyds reports were bequeathed for the John Jefferies Collection by my late, loveable cousin, Gerald Beadle, the only son of gentleman Jack Beadle, gentleman and scholar. All these works, as the fabulous programme Hornblower, would indeed make fantastic filming of our heritage and that of America. This would be a joy for the world to share.

Captain Tom Diaper - as a family we spent many happy hours with this superb sailorman. Much time was spent in his home and also in Mr. Green's old riverside café/tobacconists at Woolston, Southampton premises, all painted with shamrock green paint. A good old, kind, river Itchen yachtsman, Captain Tom Diaper was appointed in 1924 sailing master of Terpsicore, later renamed Lulworth, but the owner had a stroke whilst out shooting and in less than two hours had passed away. So the master and crew were all paid off, including Bill Braden, a mariner who served and raced on board Meteor and Shamrock, racing in America in 1920 serving as an officer on board the 23-metre Shamrock. Captain Tom Diaper served as mate and sailed across to America on board the same Shamrock, of which his sailing master brother, Alf Diaper, was in command on the 15th February 1920. They prepared her to cross the Atlantic; to act as trial horse for Shamrock IV, which was already over there sailing in 1914 when war came on. The brilliant 1st Mate to serve the 23-metre Shamrock in 1920 was Jim Gilby of Bosham in Hampshire. His brother, Jeff, was also a remarkable sailorman. My favourite books to enjoy reading are Tom Diapers Log, and the book 'Come and Sail', by a former yachtsman of the river Itchen, J.S. Hughes, who incidentally was very much involved with Endeavour in 1937, being a mariner serving on board M K Viva II, not forgetting a good engineer, the late Mr. Les Bishop, a local man, who served as electrician on board Viva. Les was a brother of the A1 brilliant sailorman, the late Stan Bishop, who served on board Endeavour in 1934. The late Stan was a very popular skipper amongst the yachting fraternity and it was a pleasure to know him all his life, being a friend and shipmate over the years.

Along with my maritime father, Stan skippered the 12-metre fantastic Yeoman class for gentleman, Mr. Aisher, for several years. I was with Stan in the gate-house of Camper & Nicholsons when he came over unwell. On going home he sadly died that night. I mention in this story, founded upon true facts, my mother and her late sister, Beatrice, who was married to my late uncle, Sid Gerrard of Northam, a man who served on board liners as fireman, and also served on Arctic convoys, MN, 2nd World War. A pattern in life like many fellow stevedores working in the docks, late uncle Sid and his friend, the late Redge Harding of Northam saved Northam from a huge inferno when incendiary bombs were dropped and burnt most fiercely in the Esso Depot yard near the Coopers Arms, very close to many houses and homes. Uncle Sid burnt his hands and clothing in doing so, whilst he was home on leave, and was highly commended by the Company, and an offer was made of a lifetime position with the Company. Their kind deed was to drive twelve lorries, which were already for delivery and were left loaded with high octane petrol, and luckily for Northam the keys were left in the ignition, thus enabling the lorries to be removed to safety.

To continue with Captain Diaper of the river Itchen who was, and still remains, in yachting circles, a living legend in his own right in the working yards which reached from the river Itchen up to the river Test and beyond. Then mad Hitler came to power and upset everyone's pattern of life with so much bombing and killing in all our big cities, and prior to starting a seafaring career after the bitter war, the memory of my pre war days still lingers within my heart, of the love and friendship that was freely given by my many relatives and family friends who resided in Northam, and around the river Itchen. The homes of many a famous mariner, not forgetting the good Hythe side of Southampton, and many a brilliant master and mariner. I myself much enjoyed talking to gentlemen mariners who served on board schooner Creole in the 1950's, Ted and John Banks and also members of the Randall family. A few years past I called to visit dear old Harry, who was skipper of the lovely Hythe Ferry for many years. On calling to see Harry, knowing the man quite well, his kind daughter said 'You have just missed Dad, he has gone out with a friend to see a new boat launched'; still very keen at 90 years of age at the time of my visit. I would also make visits to the home of the late Harry 'Jumbo' Randall who was one of the jovial crew members in 1937 to sail on board Endeavour, including making visits to see sailorman Robert Parker, of the river Itchen, Endeavour No. 2. mastheadsman and being a very proud man A1 rigger: Robert, thank you sir for my fantastic bell rope presented to me.

The lovely, strongly built, rivetted passenger boats were first class, built by the Ironworks at Rowhedge and are still of a good working service in Southampton. Many yacht masters were top sailormen and brilliant navigators in the heyday of the big class yachts of sail and steam.

The late captain Tom Felton still lives on as a household name of both senior and junior of Southampton and USA. There was the late captain Fred Stokes of Tollesbury who made his home with his family in Southampton. Captain Durham, master mariner whose brilliant son, A1 first class mariner, holding extra masters qualifications at the young age of 24 in 1932, when he was serving 2nd mate on board Lord and Lady Iliffe's magnificent schooner, Radiant ex Xarifa. Five Tollesbury mariners were proud to sail with this happy go lucky gentleman who spoke in my company and said 'We would trust our lives and sail through hell and high water with such a brilliant sailorman, navigator'. All the facts, plus all the photographs and names of crew members, nationwide, are within the JJ collection, with a tribute to members of the Randall families. Hythe side of Southampton, like the river ltchen, is quite quaint with plenty of untold stories of the sea to tell, as my old recordings, found in a local cupboard, will tell. Praying the forgotten maritime heritage is vital to the good folk of the Hythe, Southampton, and PC John Randell, gentleman of the Cowes Division Police, with whom I enjoyed a nautical a yarn at the Southampton Boat Show in 1996, pointing out to me respected river police, in my photographs; men who showed me much respect in my yachting days.

Valkyrie II, was sunk by Santanita. Captain John Thomas Randall piloted the ill-fated vessel. Tom was also a household name around the Hythe and river ltchen. Tom, the elder brother of Sam, mastered the Cuckoo in succession of many of our best racing captains. He, also mastered Stephenie 20 Pater, built at Cowes, Isle of Wight, from MY Clayton's designs for a syndicate, of which Prince Batthyany was the head, Tom and Sam Randall, being natives of the Hythe, resided in a pair of lovely cottages in a rural lane not far from the shore, close to the pretty yachting residence of Mr. T.B. C. West, the builder of the celebrated 40-rater, Queen Mab, which captain Ben Parker mastered for many racing seasons, with mainly Diaper and Parker crew members, as the JJ collection can prove. Captain Ben also, over the yachting seasons, mastered Queen Mab, 40-rater, and all along the river ltchen the clan congratulated him when H.M Kaiser William, Emperor of Germany, appointed captain Ben as sailing master to take command of Meteor. The crew, in 1900, were mostly river ltchen mariners. To name a few:- Diapers, Parkers, Drapers, Alf Candy, Bradens and many more household names along the river ltchen. Captain James Harrison of the Alern Line was a much-respected navigator who had sailed with many of the river ltchen mariners, and had also served on board Valkyries as navigators.

In 1905 with the full crew sitting around the deck on board Meteor, as my kind readers can tell, a photograph that hung in a warm and friendly maritime home, along the river ltchen, the mark proves it hung upon a rusty nail for many years. One good sailorman upon this photograph, I am led to believe, and have no doubts, that my maritime father, and my grand old shipmate, the late Bill Braden from the river ltchen, was a crew member. (I stand corrected if proved otherwise JJ). Also on the photograph is the elder brother, named William Parker, little Richard Parker being murdered and cannibalised on the high seas: (Yacht Mignonette story May 1884, full family facts within the, JJ collection).

So, my kind readers, from the river Itchen, with the ebb tide, I will now skull back to the Hythe side of the Solent. Sam and Tom Banks were born fishermen and served Meteor as officers over the racing seasons. Tom was four years older than Sam, first seeing the light of day on May 9th 1846. Tom's first yacht was the Silver Fish, gentleman owner, Mr. Jessop of the Hythe. Ted Banks Snr., of the Hythe, was skipper. Tom sailed as mate with skipper Jack Wyatt, this was the first promotion from before the mast when he served on board Arethusa racing, owned by Mr. Thomas Goodwood. Tom also served with skipper Jem Banks. Captain John Thomas Randall took command of the 90-ton Veronica ketch, owned by gentleman Mr. Freak. He spent five years working ashore in the yacht yards and fishing, and always managed to fit in some pilot positions racing, and during the Solent Regattas his vessels winning two cups, one which was taken by Valkyrie I, in the Royal Southern Match, from Calshot round the Isle of Wight against Ivernia, Blue Rock, Maid Marian and three forty-raters. The other cup was from the Royal Yacht Squadron Match of 1892 when the Cosair managed to save her time from H. M the German Emporer's Meteor. The finish caused great excitement. He also piloted Deirdre, a twenty-rater, during the 1893 racing season for the Earl of Dunraven under another brilliant sailing master of Rowhedge, Essex, captain Lemon Cranfield, and also the illfated Valkyrie II.

During my maritime father's seafaring career Dad had also served on board SY Tuscarora under the command of Captain Lemon Cranfield sailing to America, in my fully cross referenced maritime writings. I pray to God our once forgotten heritage is not just vital to our maritime nation but all good folk around the world with a love of heritage.

In 1937 my maritime father was a serving crew member on board Sunbeam [II] under the command of a company A1 master and mariner, gentleman captain Nicholas, and took part in .Round the Islands Race in Canada. Also serving as jovial shipmates from locally were the late Mr. Charles Branch, Mr. George (Knocker) Peggs and Mr Charles Hempsted.

Back to Shamrocks and Valkyries, my parents' landlord was Mr. Ernest Field, who lived in Nelson Street, Brightlingsea.

And the rent to be paid was 2/9d per week.
One of my jobs was to take the rent
across to this kind and gentle, red-faced old gent.
For in his workshop hundreds of hours spent,
and mother always jokingly told me that I took
a long time to pay the rent!
His shipwright tools were highly polished, each
had it's place
for these he had treasured and carried,
when on Valkyries and Shamrocks he did race.

He made me my first bucket and spade to play with
on the sea shore
but, deep inside, I'm sorry that I don't have them
any more.
With eyes so blue and straight he used to tell me
stories so true
and he always wore Valkyries' Guernseys and cap
of navy blue.
He talked of old racing cutter Bloodhound and said
'Not far from your feet
there are three of her old sailors who lived just
down our street
there was William Godfrey and his brother-in-Law
George Siret
to name but two. Robert Howe senior who lived in
our street too.'
Captain Sycamore was in command of Valkyries.
Charley and Jack Wilkins of Rowhedge 87 and 85
respectively in 1987
their good father being a Valkyries sailor. And Mr.
Brown was
their mother's brother. A serving sailor crushed to
death below.
When Satanita gave her such a mighty blow.
Late Captain Ned Heard of Tollesbury served
Bloodhound as well
and his brother Jack as mastheadsman where, from
over 100 feet,
tragically he fell.
Alas, the crew had lost a wonderful pal.
Another sailor from Tollesbury was Willie Michael,
who served as well,
William Gager - for 11 years as second mate he did
sail old Bloodhound, and Frank and Sid Heard's
father for 17 years served as well.

He owned the smack, Sunbeam, she looks lovely
when sailing,
but his brother Frank - his hobby was wildfowling.
For many an hour in his punt he did sit
and often, in winter, his bum froze to it!
It was a joy to live in Nelson Street, Captain Joseph
French
he was one of the best
and as a boy I worked in the river Colne with this
gent and the rest.

The mast of old Bloodhound still stands so proudly
at the Royal Yacht Squadron at Cowes for all to see
the cutter, L'Esperance ran down the old
Bloodhound in 1908
Captain Chaplin did serve along with good sailors
all now of late.
When I was a young lad, just very small
my late uncle, Jack Beadle, owned the loveliest
barge of them all.
For 18 years he mastered this great dame
The Lord Kitchener - that was her name.
Coal was after her load, and dirt - there wasn't a
spot she looked less like a barge, but more like a
yacht! From the river Itchen came the Diapers and
Parkers two good families which produced some
famous yacht masters.
They sailed most every famous yacht to sail the sea
and Horace Parker, eleven years mate of the barge,
was uncle to me.

Both uncles, being extremely kind
but not a more happy pair could anyone find
but whilst tacking up the Solent, homeward bound
they sped in 1936
alas, the main-sheet block struck Uncle Horace on
the head.
My father served on Lord and Lady Fairhaven's SY,
58 the crew
SY Sapphire RYS my father served for five
seasons.

Our Southampton cousins were fifty eight in all
and four were Parkers, all very small.
Jack, Norman, Roy and Lydia.
My brother and I were often at play
at 1, Tramway Cottages, Northam for most of the day.
Our auntie Chris was so very kind
with all the noise she never did mind.
With all of the kids making such a din
she would only laugh, and then join in! .

The tragic element of going to sea
is that many a door is knocked on, bringing grief and misery
as, instead of arriving home as usual, happy as could be
his body would be fetched home - as dead as he could be.

One year later, down at Southampton again
alas, we had suffered tragedy the same,
For Ali and Jackie Bell.
they are both cousins to me.
Their father was a regular fireman on many a ship
until on the deck of the Empress of Britain he did slip,
Liner Canadian Pacific Line,
the distance between decks, he did fall
a total of 90 feet in all.
From this fall, on his feet he did land
(My uncle he was always kind and grand).
eleven fluent languages he could speak in
And a better position he had been seeking.
He was due to become an interpreter on this ship
until he had that unfortunate slip.

On his back, in a Southampton General hospital, for 2 years he did lay
and blessed doctors and staff 'til his dying day.
As the Empress of Britain slid beneath the waves
she took many a mariner to a watery grave.
On hearing the sad news, which upset him most of all.
(From West End in Southampton).
through the night, to the docks, five miles he did crawl.
on board this liner, good shipmates - he lost many.
during his long stay in hospital they shared every penny.
But when his shipmates perished in the ocean so deep
my uncle for many a night could not sleep.

My auntie Nora struggled to bring up two children small,
relatives and crew members of this liner were kindest of all.
My uncle lingered on until 1968
when God finally opened the Golden Gate.

As a small child, only six years old
my happiness could not be bought with gold.
We resided in Mill Street, just of Hurst Green,
where the neighbours
one and all were so very kind
But when my mother was offered a much better house, she said 'I don't mind'.
Mr. Day, with his lovely horses and cart
helped mother, from the Green to depart.
On arrival at Nelson Street, she said, 'Oh Dear! Mr. Day what can I do?
I have only five shillings and two!'
In reply he said for good neighbour like you
this will do'.

Mr. Day & Son's with horses, and his hearse
polished from bottom to top
they looked so magnificent - infact as smart as any yacht!

Now we lived in Nelson Street with kind neighbours short and tall
and from the names as Valkyries, Shamrock, Bloodhound, Westward,
Lulworth and Brittania as well, on their jerseys, you could tell
they had sailed on board them all.
If one only had in those days a recorder what a wonderful story
it could tell.

(Fully cross-referenced, river Itchen as well JJ)

'Granny Wheeler' lived next door
a very close friend and our neighbour.
Large numbers of the Wheeler family perished at sea.
including the two she loved best, who perished in tragedy.
Her master mariner husband whilst working on a 6,600 ton wooden
walled ship on a run job from Portsmouth to Maldon, Essex
on November 29th 1924 along with other good sailors
when beneath the waves tragically they did slip.
In 1926, Ernest Wheeler joined the schooner Westward
and when captain Frederick Davis, owner, asked him to make new masts, he said that he would
William Aldous was the brilliant mate on board
And for 26 years he faithfully served
Captain Davis did all the swearing, Captain Alf Diaper hardly
swore a word
Captain Frederick Wheeler and Captain Simmons
aged 54 and 67 of Brightlingsea perished
November 1924

(With all photographs in full JJ Collection).

Mr. Ernest Field, my parents' landlord, served
Valkyries in 1895
with Captain John Thomas Randall from
Southampton - to be precise,
the Home Hythe.
Whilst racing, the Satanita crashed into Valkyrie's
port side
but the Captain, Captain J. T. Randall piloting
wasn't at the helm at the time.
It was Lord Dunraven who sat there - but no one
was to blame.
a passenger boat, from the stern of a the yacht, did
appear
Captain Cook Diaper of the Itchen on Satanita came
about to steer clear
As Mr. Brown of Rowhedge was working below
he was crushed to pieces from the mighty blow.
Ashore in Scotland, he sadly died
Captain William Cranfield, all night, sat by his side.
Captain Edward Isaac Sycamore, who was in
command
and 1st mate Mr. Cranfield of Rowhedge and all of
the crew
did donate one week's wages to his widow and
dependants
the best they could do.

Captain Edward Isaac Sycamore, a world renowned sailing master was called to higher circles on April 9th 1930 in his 74th year, his respected wife, Rosetta, with whom I often enjoyed a nautical discussion who joined him on September 24th 1962 in her 101st year. May God bless them both.

Although I was born in Brightlingsea there is much
I have written about the sea
and pray to God that some day you can all read
what it means to me.
Many people were injured, and many lives were
saved
but the sad part of 'going to sea' - many suffered a
watery grave.
The work was hard and the pay was small
In my works, complete with photographs, I name
them all.

Being born on the 15th July 1929 and proud to know I was Christened in All Saints Church, Northam Road, Southampton, where my parents were wed on the 8th October 1928, known as Happy Northam.

I do believe in the Good-Lord above and owning all the good mariners' photographs nationwide I pray that He will bear witness and bless each and every one with his love.

YACHT SEVEN SEAS. EX ABRAHAM RYDBURGH A CONVERTED BARQUENTINE.

My friend late Jack Felton and Sailorman Charlie Rasmussen, who was a brilliant Danish seaman and was known as Smiler. Jack Felton served his shipwrights apprenticeship in Aldous Shipyard after the 1st World War when for 18 years Jack's maritime father, Captain Tom Felton Snr. master mariner, mastered SY Lorna for owner the late Sir Walter Preston MP. (For approx. 18 years.) He also mastered motor yacht Tiger. The kind owner sadly died in 1936.

Jack's master mariner brother, the late Captain Tom Felton, famous yacht master. He served Sam Speagels' yacht, Malarne, in England and the USA. He also mastered American Passenger Liners SS Emerald Isle and Liner Jamaica Queen. Captain Tom Felton Jnr. passed away in his Miami home, USA in December 1992 aged 96 years.

Captain Tom Felton Snr., on the third day of World War II, said his farewells to our family upon the mainline Southampton railway station, and we travelled back home to Brightlingsea along with fellow yachtsmen, the late Mr. Frank Hempstead and Mr. Alan Salmon. I must add within my story the late businessman, Mr. Fred House. He was a most kind man and very often fetched my father and fellow yachtsmen home, with luggage and kit bags sitting on top of the milk churns, whilst collecting milk from the railway station, pre-Second World War.

Late Captain Arthur Felton owned the Bawely fishing smack, Helen & Violet, pre-second World War. This well preserved fishing smack was owned by gentleman Mr. John Walsh who always greets my fellow friend, late sailorman Jack Felton, and I with most kind greetings, also a good nautical yarn. The late sailorman, Stan Felton, a brother of Jack was also a seafaring gentleman. Captain Arthur Felton fished out of Leigh being a first rate yachtsman and fisherman; a pattern in life, like many Essex fellow mariners. His home, number 3, Southsea Avenue, Southend. He piloted all the large racing cutters over the many racing seasons during the big events, regattas, starting racing from Southend pier. Captain Felton was known and respected by my maritime father and also he was known by my late Uncle, Harold Stroud, of Whitstable in Kent, who was the 1st Mate on board the R.R. Cutter, Britannia, from 1931 until 1936. Captain Felton became pier master at Southend around 1945 and he was called to higher circles in approximately the 1950s. It was also very upsetting for all yacht owners, fellow yachtsmen, and the most tragic news for all the family and the folk of our small community at that time, with a very small population in our Cinque Port Town when George Henry Lewes drowned from the big yacht Astra, with most families involved with the sea, or working in the shipyards. During the Second World War 750 men, women and boys were in Aldous shipyard. My clocking in number was 141, working as a plumber's lad upon many vessels with the late friend, G.G. Holland. I must add it was most upsetting at times to see destruction to vessels and human beings that served at sea during war. God bless all their memories many of which photographs are within the JJ collection.

Dad had during the 1927/1928 yachting season's had the honour to serve on board Sir John and Lady Thorny Crofts Dutch barge yacht, Joyeen. RYS Skipper, Jack Cook Snr., Mate, William Goff and Sailorman Fred Death, made up the jovial crewmembers.

The late skipper, Percy Howe, my skipper in 1947, being a very kind and helpful-natured person who loved talking of the lovely, famous Endeavours, of which he was a crewmember 1934 and 1937, he also served the 12 metre Flicka in 1938: His wishes, along with his charming Tollesbury wife, was retirement at Lymington, being his dream home. The late Lord Camrose being, our rich owner, was better known as Sir William Berry, the newspaper magnate of the Daily Telegraph. The 2nd Viscount, Sir John Seymour Berry (TD) of Hackwood Park, in the County of Southampton, (a younger brother of Trinity House), also Baron Camrose of Long Cross was born 12.7.1909 and succeeded his father, as 2nd Viscount in 1954, Vice CDRE of the Royal Yacht Squadron who was born 23.6.1849, created a Baronet 4.7.1921, raised to the Peerage as Baron Camrose of Long Cross, Surrey. His Lordship died 15.6.54 and was succeeded by his eldest son. As previously mentioned, myself, as a yearly crewmember, served AB Hack boatman, meaning the working launch. Before the Second World War the late Lord Camrose proudly sailed and raced his famous J Class racing cutter, Cambria, and at the same time owned the grand 500 tonne MY Sonia: This vessel was mastered by a very good deep-sea master and gentleman, Captain Merrifield of Southampton, and his son, who had served as Coxswain in the University boat race. Also I must mention the 1st Mate of SY Sonia who was Mr. Beteridge. Chief Engineer, MY Noyce, Chef Lew Lake, River Itchen, regular crewmembers who I believe were on board SY Sonia, under the Admiralty, when she was lost in war off Portland. Like all other rich gentlemen, they had the large motor yachts to assist on fine weather when their large racing cutters were becalmed, to tow them sometimes in order to reach their destination on time from the Clyde to Harwich or vice versa. However, for reasons unknown, it is understood by men of the racing cutters that MY Sonia never did tow the late Lord Camroses' J class Cambria to commence racing. The late Skipper Alec Goff, local, served the Cambria as Mast Headsman No. I, and he sailed about the world with dad in 1925 on board the 500 tonne schooner Kallisto, and in 1926 on board 24 metre Lulworth.

The MY Virginia had started to fit out and take on her 28 crew, plus a Marconi sparks, on sailing. We would sail for the Med each year for a cruise and I found this yacht a remarkable vessel to sail upon. Our good chief engineer looked after the 12 twin-screw cylinder saucer diesel engines, like he would his grandfathers gold watch, and being signed on as AB launchman myself the chief would always, at Cowes South, or any other port of call abroad when the motor boats were in use, would come to see the two launchmen and kindly enquire as to our health and also the health of the launch engines. During my long stay I found our chief engineer a most pleasant man at all times, being the late Mr. Johnny Nye of Wooleston, Southampton and he kindly gave me a £1 note after every cruise on landing at Southampton and would thank me kindly for taking good care of the launch engine. Then he would smile and say thank you Bricklesea.

On board the 750 ton MY Virginia we carried on the boat deck 5 boats in all; these being the owner's launch which was 24ft long, of Victorian style, and capable of 20 knots; The crew's launch was 18ft long and capable of 9 knots; A sailing cutter, which was 20ft long, and was used mostly as a hack boat to clean the yacht's sides. A 20ft speed boat was on deck, but very seldom used, and a lovely 14ft yacht's sailing dinghy, with all the heavy brasswork, on board the Virginia, cleats, bollards and hoisting winches, and with all the teak varnish work. It would take us AB's three hours scrubbing down to clean each morning, chammy up and get all the bright work clean. It was at this time useful practice to clean oneself up after work ready for boat work. At first we carried on board the Sailors' Bibles, Holy Stones, and our good Boatswain, Mr. Pitt, would always make the crew sing to Sally Army tune of 'Bringing in the Sheaves' and we had to sing the Holy Stone song whilst sliding them up and down the lovely decks. The song went:

Fetch little buckets of water,
Spreading the grains of sand,
Pushing a bloody great Holy Stone.
Makes the decks look grand.
Push you rotten sinners,
You're working under me
And when you get my decks clean,
How happy I will be.

But our late Boatswain Mr. Ted Pitt, DSM of Wivenhoe South, was the best shipmate anyone could wish to serve under. He was a brilliant seaman and rigger and well respected by all who ever had the pleasure of working and sailing with him. His final working days were spent cycling to and from his 415, Burgess Road, Swaything home for 6 years, serving as a brilliant rigger in Camper & Nicholson's, Northam.

We had some fantastic cruises such as Scotland, Ireland, West Indies, Normandy Beaches and all Northern France, Mediterranean cruising, all the Spanish Ports, Balearic Islands, Corsican Islands and all ports of Corsica and Southern France, also the Arctic Circle (the fabulous land of the midnight sun) with the late Duke of Westminster for four months in 1951. Lord Camrose enjoyed his privacy and spoke very little to his crew, but we were very well provided for and as I recall in all my happy cruising hours on board this vessel, Lord Camrose spoke to me but once only. We were approaching Calvi, Corsica and went to anchor on approaching our anchorage Position. The late Captain Behenna called out to our ship's carpenter, late John Bragg, who had relieved 'Chippy' Ike Martin of Wooleston South. The captain said "stand by, this is deep water, let go the starboard anchor at 15 fathoms and hold. When I tell you, give her 30 fathoms in the water." However, I stood with John Bragg of local, to assist the ships carpenter, and the brake on the starboard windlass barrel did not hold when the 15-fathom ran out. The anchor and chain just kept running and at the 30 fathom shackle it whip lashed into the air, almost hit John and I on the head, and flew down and out of the horse pipe never to be seen again Whilst laying stern to in Cannes harbour, where the big yachts were laying, one of the yachts wanted to get under way and had a fouled anchor cable. They had a diver go down to break and clear the chain, and it was presumed he could have removed our shackle pin at the 30 fathom mark by mistake and did not report the dangerous error. This almost cost us our lives. John Bragg, after our cruise, was most fortunate of being shipped up as the ships carpenter on board the troop ship SS Empire Orwell.

However, to continue the story: Lord Camrose departed to the shore and on his return to the yacht, there were quite a few items to come on board, at the owner's starboard gangway, out of the owner's launch; This was generally carried out by the Stewards, but as we were to get under way immediately I was sent to help, in order that we could get the launch hoisted quickly up and stowed on the boat deck. After cleaning the deck the crew was not permitted aft of the deck, unless ordered to do so by the late captain Behenna, or 1st mate. Lord Camrose had seen me helping with the items and launch, and on my way back round the aft poop deck his Lordship spoke to me thus 'Where are you from lad?' and for a joke I replied 'Foc'le Sir'. 'No, no, no man,' he replied, 'home place?' 'Brightlingsea, Sir.' 'Ha ha ha - only been there once in my life, with my two yachts, MY Sonia and J Class Cambria.' Whilst Mediterranean cruising off Algiers we also received a Mayday call from the troop ship Empire Windrush, but our assistance was not required.

My maritime father, having sailed the world under sail and steam on board world famous yachts along' with world famous yacht owners, yachting prior to outbreak of the 1st World War and soon after the bloody war was over, but sadly never over for many poor souls who fought in battle for their country. My father, like many fellow mariners destroyed many famous old photographs and discharge books. As a lad, when visiting maritime homes along the River Itchen and in Brightlingsea, upon the walls was our maritime heritage. Whilst on a Cowes, Isle of Wight visit 1997 by chance, just strolling down Artic Road, passing the house where my late auntie and uncle resided, Auntie Edith and Uncle Harold Stroud, 1st mate to serve the royal racing cutter Britannia 1931-6. A maritime point of interest, prior to joining Britannia my uncle was the mate on August 4th 1931 on board the 12 metre Lucilla when run down by the mammoth 24 metre racing cruiser Lulworth; my uncle saving captain Deakens life. Sadly, W. Saunders was trapped below, and sailorman Mr. Ashby of Burnham on Crouch was a survivor. Whilst walking with my friend Ken Wheeler down Artic Road a gentleman remarked 'you look like yachties.' I politely replied 'we only know a little about past yachting sir.' So he said 'look here my boys at what hangs in my garage.' And it was a photograph of all the 50-odd crewmembers on board the old steam yacht SY Tuscarora of which captain Candy, of the river Itchen, was in command after the ship had seen war service during the 1st World War, and sailed out of Aldous dock, local. This was after being refitted after the war and then sailing to America with many local crewmembers. Captain Candy, Admiral Commander Candy, was a 1st World War submarine commander and hero. He lost a submarine, and only 2 or 3 crewmembers survived, I believe a Cowes, Isle of Wight man named Mr. Sid Spicer was the elderly gentleman to have shown Ken and I the photograph after wiping the cobwebs and dust half away. He said 'look my boys, this was yachting in the good old days. And look, this man was my father who served on SY Tuscarora as the 4th engineer in around 1919.' So it aroused my curiosity and I asked Mr. Spicer to wipe the other side of this lovely old photograph, and there, lo and behold, I said politely 'yes, and here is my maritime father.' This is one photograph and so unique, but a copy was sent to me as promised: Strange, but true. A first rate marine engineer who has been called to rest, aged almost 90 years in 1999, meaning Mr. Les Lazell, who worked on Admiralty ships in Aldous shipyard during the 2nd World War. He also served yachting and he always would say, in conversation with myself, that when he was just a lad he stood at the end of Aldous shipyard dock and said a prayer for SY Tuscarora, also her crewmembers, for a safe voyage across the Atlantic.

My father never spoke much about his experiences in life, plus world travels under sail and steam, but he spoke often of local mariners and sailormen. Those who he had been shipmates with, and respected Late Bill Woodward, yachtsman of Wivenhoe, Skipper owner of CK Prima Donna, Captain James Barnard, who as a seaman was a shipmate of my father on board SY Sayonara of which he named his Rowhedge cottage. As previously mentioned Rowhedge Captains William Cranfield and Lemon Cranfield, whom dad highly respected and sailed with. Late sailorman, Harry Parker of Rowhedge, a most jovial man who skippered the ML converted yacht, Rosabelle II, after the 2nd World War. Not forgetting my maritime fathers friends and shipmates, the good sailormen brothers Ted, Harry and Bill Hilliyard, being most brilliant sailormen who served and sailed on board many famous yachts, following a family tradition. Henry Hilliyard was captain of the steam yacht SY Edwina, which used to sail from Rowhedge between 1883 and 1901. His sons, Ted, Harry and Bill served on the SY Rosabelle, Shamrock IV, SY Sayonara, RRC Britannia, SY Sapphire, SY Heliopolis and SY Iolanda. Captain Henry Hilliyard later in life ran the Rowhedge to Wivenhoe ferry. He held his Master Mariners qualifications and, like myself, he was a Freeman of the River Colne of Royal Charter Birthrights. He was called to rest 2.9.1912 aged only 62 years. Alfred E Chaplin from Southampton, whom I met by chance, is a grandson of Captain Henry Hilliyard, and holds fondest memories from his youth and holidays spent at Rowhedge, being his mothers' birthplace, and where his mother attended the mariners' chapel regularly. On the 21.8.99, Open Day and Fair, All Saints Church, Brightlingsea; a Church known throughout the world as the Mariners' Church. Part of the JJ collection was exhibited to help with the 'save our tower' appeal. My gratitude is given to those who show respect towards myself and my lifetime's maritime recordings, Sacred To All Their Memories.' It was just great to have my close, sailorman friend, world travelled mariner, late Jack Felton, aged 94 years, a guest with us for the weekend, Jack recalling his apprenticeship days in Aldous shipyard after the 1st

World War. Jack was a scout leader, 2nd troop in Brightlingsea from 1918-1936. My thanks to the kind gentleman, Mr. Harold Lord, local reporter, for a welcome report on my friend Mr. Jack Felton's seafaring career. My gratitude is expressed in full to gentleman historian and author, Mr. Claude Dove, also the mariners who greeted and welcomed sailorman Jack Felton on the 21st August 1999 at All Saints Church open day and fair. My friends, skipper Malcolm McGregor and Clacton lifeboat coxswain and RN during the 2nd World War, Richard Harman. Mr. Brian and Mrs. Carol Green, retired fish & chip business couple from Wivenhoe. Brian's grandfather, Friday Green, mariner and navigator, served on board the royal racing cutter, Britannia, as navigator 1904 onwards, also racing in the Mediterranean under Captain John Carter's command. This Rowhedge sailing master, being the father of Mrs. Gladys White, and brother of the late skipper Alfred Carter. Strange but true, as the old photographs can prove. My father's uncle, 'Tarts' (a nickname) Henry Brasted, served several seasons as 2nd mate on board Britannia and was also a Valkyrie sailorman. Mr. T. Wright, chief engineer, retired, and friend of JJ, also Mr. Ron and Mrs. Myrna Atkinson, Ron was our Town Deputy. It was a joy for my friend Jack to receive such a welcome in the Cinque Port Town he so loves, as he was also a long friend of a much-respected lady, Mrs. Gladys White, the mother of gold medallist Mr. Reg White and his sister Pam. Jack took a very special bouquet of flowers and, with warm affection, placed them on Gladys' grave.

Sacred to all their memory, to keep all their memories alive.

ROYAL RACING CUTTER BRITANNIA R.Y.S. 1904 - 1908

Royal Racing Cutter Britannia R.Y.S. 1921. East Coast crew members (Tolesbury, Wivenhoe, Brightlingsea). Foreground, Her majesty Queen Mary, to her right His Majesty King George V.

A regular serving 2nd mate was my grandmother's brother, William Edward Brasted, known as 'Tarts Brasted'. He appears in many old famous photographs. A well kept secret in those days from his own family and the media, and witnessed by William Brasted, and was only spoken of after his death, was that after the finish of a days racing during Cowes Week, H.M. King Edward VII challenged H.I.M. Kaiser William to a race in the Cutter, Sailing and Rowing boats. Yacht tenders Kaiser William Meteor, under the command of Captain Ben Parker of the River Itchen, apparently won. Upon landing on the steps at the Royal Yacht Squadron first, H.I.M. Kaiser William jeered at King Teddy as to the result. Straight away King Teddy punched him in the mouth and knocked him down, and stormed into the Yacht Club. William Brasted witnessed this episode whilst standing in the beaten Racing Cutter. Captain John Carter, M.V.O. and Bar, serving master at the time, was on board the Royal Racing Cutter. Captain Carter died in 1910 aged 50 years, William Brasted, My maritime father's uncle, served on shamrocks and valkyries.

Lord Dunraven, being an Irish Lord and Gentleman, paid higher wages than on board British owned yachts. Come the year 1913-14 Lord Dunraven greatly respected the knowledge of oysters, the cultivating and breeding of which our family were well conversed, owning our own freehold ground rights and leasehold ground rights in the north and south channel and around underwood's, hard plus Lynch Creek. However, William Brasted, being R.N.V.R., could not accept the very kind offer made to him by Lord Dunraven to manage his oyster beds and pits in County Cork. Sailorman William Brasted died in 1934 aged 54 years.

H.M. Kind Edward VII, a much loved king, was greatly respected by all of his crew members. The same respects were held towards Lord Dunraven and also towards H.I.M. Kaiser William, who, on the outbreak of the First World War, gave all internees, yacht masters, officers and sailormen safe passage back to England.

Enclosed photograph, Meteor Crew, taken on board in 1905 whilst yacht laid in Hamburg, Germany. All River Itchen crewmembers.

Three serving Parker brothers, Captain Ben Parker, 1st mate Daniel Parker and 2nd mate Bill Parker. Captain Ben Parker was grandfather of my uncle Horace Parker who was killed on board my uncle Jack Beadles' sailing barge, Lord Kitchener, in 1936. Sailorman William Parker, being the elder brother of little Richard Parker, murdered and cannibalised on the high seas (yacht Mignonette story).

When this photograph was kindly allowed for the JJ Collection it was removed from a rusty nail within a warm and friendly River Itchen maritime home. Some crewmembers were household names, Diapers, Matthews, Bradens, Candies and many more, who were brilliant sailormen. Dear old Bill Braden was a Meteor sailorman who I feel honoured not only to have known but also to have sailed with.

In 1952 Bill was one of our serving crewmembers on board Lord Viscount Camrose's Luxury Yacht, M.Y Virginia of the R.Y.S. Bill serving as owner's launchman. Captain Ben Parker was indeed the first sailing master to be appointed sailing master on board Meteor and was congratulated by all the clan along the River Itchen.

Upon the third day of the second World War, Mrs Parker, being skipper Ben Parker (Juniors's) kind wife, and four young children, came to say there farewells to our family. On leaving Northam to come home to Brightlingsea, this lovely kind lady and three of her children, at their River Itchen home were tragically killed on the first day of the air raid on the city of Southampton: One of the daughters, who is known and respected by J.J., was saved by running on an errand for her mother. My prayers are for all.

William Aldous, of Colne Road, Brightlingsea, Essex:

Recorded Service of a most brilliant man of sail the late

1895 Sailing Vessel Neptune

1895 Aged 21, position Mate

1896 Schooner Daphne as Mate

1897 Vigilant USA

1899 Ailsa as Mate

1900 Vililant USA

1901 Shamrock II

1902 - 1903 Bona as Mate

1904 - 1905 Cicely as Mate

1907 - 1908 Schooner as Mate

1910 - 1913 White Heather as Mate

1914 - 1918 Served at sea

1919 - 1920 Yachting

1921 joined famous racing schooner Westward as 1st mate and served faithfully until 1947, then he left to join the schooner Moonbeam as mate with skipper Harry Wade and jovial Brixham sailors.

Above: William Aldous.

Left: Captain John Carter of Rowhedge and Henry (Tarts) Brasted. On board Royal Racing Cutter Britannia 1904.

SIR JOHN ISAAC THORNEYCROFT. FRS
(1843 - 1928)

Sir John Thorneycroft was a great pioneer in naval architecture. The advances he made in hull design and machinery of small high-speed craft served to show what could be done in larger vessels. A most remarkable, neat draughtsman and his line drawings were works of art. In 1916 he invented Motor Torpedo Boats or Scooters, which were used in raids on Zebrugge and Ostend. He died at the age of 85 on the 28th June 1928 at Bembridge, Isle of Wight, where he also had a home, Steyne House.

During the 1926 yachting racing seasons my maritime father served and raced on board the famous 24-metre racing cruiser, Lulworth, under the command of the late Captain Charles Bevas of the River Itchen. My father was one of the twenty-six serving crew members and in this very special racing season on board, the late gentlemen, and Sir M Singer's fabulous yacht, the crew won more prize money than taking wages. My maritime father's pattern in life was sailing the world on board many famous yachts. His life had been hard, like most mariners, (He was a POW during the 1st World War in Germany) fishing, yachting, escalloping and some winter months working in the pickling yards after having to scull the loaded skiffs ashore from the Tollesbury and Wivenhoe smacks to the Brightlingsea yard, with masters and owners who were most jovial and were all brilliant yachtsman and fishermen.

My most treasured gift in life was my own yachting career and sailing with many of my father's respected grand old shipmates from Essex, Southampton and also from the Cornish villages. My lovable grandparents, Alfred and Florence Harfield of 8, Lower York Street in Northam, Southampton, as at one time those proud old happy homes stood until the early 1960s. These homes I knew quite well as a lad and the folk who dwelt within these walls including many good kind folk who lost loved ones on board RMS Titanic. This was pre Second World War days when my father sailed the world on board SV Sapphire RYS, a luxury yacht with fifty eight private crew-members. It was commanded by a gentleman, Captain Reveley of Southampton, followed by Captain Stan Gilbert of Brightlingsea. My Northam born and bred mother had served at sea on board liners, working in the laundry department. At one time I had thirty eight aunties and uncles and fifty eight cousins, who mostly all resided around Northam and the glorious River Itchen, which came into my seafaring and yachting career, also sailing out of the brilliant yacht yard, Camper & Nicholsons. Now renamed Shamrock Quay.

I often think of my dearly departed Northam uncles. They had sailed the world at sea MN and RN. With our own maritime tragedies, we had quite a few within our family.

So back to 1927: The late skipper Jack Cook senior of Brightlingseas served yacht Joyeen. This was a fabulous yacht, owned by Sir J.I. Thorneycroft, who was highly respected by his local crew-members; only four in all. The Captain, Goff of Brightlingsea, was the serving mate. He was a Shamrock sailorman in 1901 and he also served Shamrock III under the command of my great Uncle, the famous Captain Robert Wringe, who passed away at his Sandy Hook home in Brightlingsea on the 14th February 1924 aged 63 years. He was born at sea, having a master mariner father. A first rate sailing master, Captain Robert was married to my grandfather's sister, Emma Jefferies. A strong point of Southampton interest, my lovable auntie Ethel, age 90, my aunties father, Jack Diaper of the river Itchen who served the mammoth Shamrocks in 1901 and 1902.

Captain William Goff was indeed a crack 40 rater racing master winning a gold medal in 1911 racing for owner A.L. Pierce, a mining engineer and owner of Carina racing against many crack masters from the River Itchen. To name but a few Parkers: Diapers,Ted, Butty, George, Shaboo, Matthew and Candy families. In the yachting season April 1927 my maritime father was shipped up to serve on board Sir John Thorneycrofts' luxury yacht along with another local seafarer as shipmate, the late Mr. Fred Death. Come October 1928 laying up time, end of the yachting season my parents were wed in St. Augustines Church, Northam, Southampton, 8th October 1928. Around the same time my lovable auntie Edith became wed to Harold Stroud of Whitstable in Kent: A very popular yachtsman, indeed, serving as first mate on board the royal racing cutter Britannia from 1931 to 1936. My Uncle Harold, much respected was born 31st January 1904 and died 6th April 1964 on the Isle of Wight. My auntie Edith was born in Northam 10th January 1905 and sadly died 21st April 1991.

Along with my mother and members of their family and school friends they sang songs of praise, and waved special flags to RMS Titanic on 10th April 1912 wishing 'God speed, and a safe voyage'. Sadly on returning to the Northam school on the Monday morning their whole neighbourhood was shattered when 140 school friends had lost a relative overnight, a father in many cases. Two Mrs. Longs, kind ladies, resided next to my grandparents their husbands, Will and Arthur both perished on board. I had the honour to know also a most quiet man who was No.1 lookout man on board Titanic, Mr. Frederick Fleet of Shirley, Southampton. He was the first man on board Titanic who spotted and reported the Iceberg. Mr Fleet would not discuss the subject all the years I knew this quiet man: Most sadly, a man who lived a living nightmare. He had a tragic ending and entered the gates of heaven on 19th June 1961. Jack Ponjesta an R.M.S. Titanic survivor married late in life, a widow Mrs Nellie Diaper whose first husband perished at sea. Friend Jack worked in the grand yacht yard Camper & Nicholsons in Northam, along with engineer Mr. George Salmon of Brightlingsea, the Salmon family being mostly local seafarers. George sailed as shipmate with my father, pre Second World War, also, just after the first world war, with a submarine commander, Capt. Candy, a hero, who mastered SY Tuscarora, which was owned by Sir W. Jennings of New York.

I often had tea with Jack and Nellie Ponjesta at their home in Curzon Court, Lordshill, Southampton. During my yachting career my favourite yacht to serve on board, as AB hack boatman from 1949 until June 1954, was M.Y. Virginia, owned by the gentleman, Lord Viscount Camrose, Commodore of the RYS, which carried 29 private crew members: Captain Behenna of St. Ives Cornwall, Wooleston, Southampton, mastered this luxury yacht. Jack Ponjesta, in all honesty, to myself only, he mentioned his living hell on one of my visits to his and Nellie's home: Jack said to me most quietly, the intensity of the noise and the screaming was unbearable until the very end when Titanic took her final plunge 2.5 miles deep; and then came the silence. Jack was ordered into one of the sixteen boats to look after and care for the women and children. Jack was called to higher circles 15th May 1968.

My dearest grandmother resided at No. 8, Lower York Street, where hundreds of workmen would walk past each day, to and from the many working yards and places of employment in and around Northam; everyone happy, everyone with a position of work. A neighbour's child was taken seriously ill and my grandmother, with her own family and problems, cared for and cured this dear child but sadly she carried the disease into her own home and her dear son, Frank Leonard Harfield ,died, aged 4 years. At his funeral, 8th March 1918 he was carried in a child's coffin of white and gilt, padded and lined with ruffled curtains and a robe. A Washington car and coach were used with a pair of horses to each of the bearers. The funeral was at Holybrook cemetery at Northam, and the fee was £5.10s. The funeral carriage was from Masters of 123 Mary Street, Southampton, doctor to the firm of John Beeston, Embalmers, Funeral Directors and Cemetery Masons.

My grandfather and grandmother, being very poor and very honest folk, paid the funeral expenses within the same week as the loss of their loved one. Over four hundred folk from Chapel and Northam followed the coach and horses on foot to the Hollybrook Cemetery for the service, including neighbours and widows for the RMS Titanic, together with young widows from the first world war. My mother's sister Nora, Mrs Bell, spent the war years as a nursing sister at the Royal Victoria Hospital, Netley, and was awarded a solid silver medal for devotion and most caring ways, and loyal duty, to save our servicemen and foe alike, in their hour of need: As did her close friend, Margery Rendall, a customs officer's daughter: Marjorie, a most attractive lady, sadly drowned in 1930 in a boating accident.

My maritime father, from his world famous yachting days along with one of his good shipmates, Alec Goff, got to know the second officer of RMS Titanic, a gentleman, Mr Lighttoller who also mastered yachts for many years, also owned his own yacht, Sundowner, now preserved at Chatham Dockyard. Mr. Lightoller, during the second World War, on board Sundowner, with the aid of small yacht patrols and fishing craft, helped to save many lives from the Normandy beaches: Also with the help of the late skipper Gerry Ashcroft of Brightlingsea, a gentleman RN, a true friend of All Saints Church, and coasting master. He passed away on 2nd June 1990 (born 22nd February 1922), a grand sailorman with whom I had the honour and privilege to sail as a shipmate. Upon skipper Gerry's headstone, 'Home is the sailor, home from the sea' and his place of worship which he so loved, All Saints Church, known as 'The Mariners' Church' to the true natives of Brightlingsea: There are many tiles on the frieze around the church walls naming our mariners who perished at sea in all parts of the world, including sailorman Mr. Conrad, Siebert, aged 30 years, a local sailorman who perished on board RMS Titanic, his brother-in-law, Reg Savage, survived the tragedy, and also the loss of a RN ship during the first world war. With sorrow J.J.'s services are no longer required, upon the Fair and Open Day, held once a year, to exhibit parts of his maritime collection, after many years of loyalty: A most bitter pill to swallow; a most unjust act. JJ was one of the founder members dedicated to saving All Saints Church. This deprives many visitors, from far and wide, of seeing the wonderful sacred tributes to our sailormen past contained in JJ's collection.

My maritime father proudly served on board Sir John Isaac's yacht, Joyeen, and served many guests during 1927 and 1928 yachting seasons. This included gentlemen Sir Thomas Sopwith who passed away January 1989 aged 101 years, respected by all serving crewmembers. He was a great pioneer and sportsman and owner of Endeavour in 1934-1937 and MY Philante in 1937.

Sir Richard Fairey of Fairey Marine, aviator and kind gentlemen, often offered to fly the Joyeen crew members home to the river Colne just to purchase some of our native oysters but they one and all refused to go in the air 'in one of those new fangled things'. Father and I being Freeman of the river Colne of Royal Charter birthrights, and with our family members owning much freehold tidal ground rights and also 1000 years royal charter leasehold rights, still not officially recognised. However, my father also greatly respected gentleman Sir William Wyndham Portal:

PORTAL. Sir William Wyndham. 2nd Bt., cr. 1901 FSA., DL., JP.

Vice lieutenant of Hampshire, Chairman of Quarter Sessions since 1928, Born 12 April 1850; e.s. son of Sir Wyndham Spencer Portal. 1st Bart., DL., JP., of Laverstoke (Lady Portal who died 1903 was the e.d. of William Hicks-Beach of Oakley, Hants); S. father, 1905; m.1880, Florence, CBE., d of Hon. St. Leger Glyn, 2nd s. of 1st Baron Wolverton; one s. one d Educ. Eaton. Christ Church, Oxford (BA 1874 MA 1876). High Sheriff 1886-7; Vice Chairman (1897-1920) and Alderman of the Hampshire County Council; late captain Hampshire Artillery Militia, Knight of Justice, Order of St. John of Jerusalem; Order of Mercy; Junior brother of Trinity House: Ex-President of the Hampshire and Isle of Wight Association of architects; Director and deputy chairman, London and South Western Railways Co., 1902-23. Owns about 800 acres. Publications: L' Eglise a Wallone (The French Huguenot Church at Southampton), 1903. The Manors and Churches of Laverstoke and freefolk in Hampshire, 1908; The Great Hall of Winchester Castle (a summary), 1916 Cowes Castle and the R.Y.S., 1918. Recreations: yachting etc., Heirs Lt. Colonel WR Portal Address: Lowerstoke House, Whitchurch Hants. Clubs. Athenaeum, Marlborough, Royal Yacht Squadron, Cowes. (Died 30 Sept. 1931).

This gentleman highly respected the loyalty of Essex yachtsmen, and in 1919, on board his fabulous sailing yacht Valdora, ten serving crew members who served on board were from Brightlingsea, under a most respected yacht master, in steam and sail, Captain Arthur Oliver. Captain Oliver was also sailing master of the racing yawl yacht Avocet: He died on board, aged 67 years, on 21st May 1931 whilst the yacht was being fitted out in Camper & Nicholsons yacht yard in Northam. The gentleman owner, Mr. Guiness, a famous merchant banker from Dublin attended his loyal Captain's funeral service, carried out in Brightlingsea. A grandson of Captain Oliver, a brilliant photographer, has remained totally loyal to my works for over 20 years. Thank you kindly dear sir, gentleman Mr. John Dalziel.

My mother was always so proud of the fact of being a Northam girl, and also proud of the fact during the end of the yachting season, 1928, she was invited by members of the Thorneycroft family to be on board yacht Joyeen for the laying up ceremony. My father was called to rest; reaching higher circles on 20th June 1970 aged 78 years. My lifetime's maritime works are, indeed, sacred to their memories.

These photographs were taken in June 1928 to commemorate the sad death of Sir John Isaac Thornycroft.
Top left: was taken on board Dutch barge yacht SV Joyeen R.S.Y. and shows the late skipper Jack Cook, Senior talking to gentleman late Sir William Portal.
Bottom left: Jack Cook, Junior, gentleman sailorman who passed away on 18th October 1994 aged 85 years, and my maritime father A. Jefferies who passed away on 20th June 1970 aged 78 years.
Right: shows my mother and late Auntie Rose, Mrs Flood, my uncles of late who were sea seafarers - Fred, Vic and Roy Harfield, standing outside Thornycroft's sail loft down Lower York Street, Northam.

350 TON SCHOONER XARIFA N.Y.Y.C.

The fabulous 380-ton schooner Xarifa NYYC was built by Samuel Whites of Cowes, Isle of Wight in 1930 for gentleman Sir Mortimor Singer, the sewing machine tycoon (with family burial vaults in Torquay, Devon). My late uncle Albert Jefferies served this yacht and her kind owner for 18 full yachting seasons. His yachts were named Xarifa. In October 1931 this magnificent schooner, master in command, Captain Dickerson of Warsash, and 1st mate, a brilliant man of sail, Bert Gladdin of Cowes, Isle of Wight, with 14 serving crew members. Upon leaving Archashan, in the bay of Biscay they struck a Mistral and Xarifa and all hands were reported missing for 10 whole days. The lutine Bell at Lloyds had been rung and the story made headline coverage and stories for two weeks following in the News of the World Newspapers.

After losing the main mast and mizzen and the owners launch, also the binnacle and compass Captain Dickerson being an A1 sailorman and navigator navigated Xarifa safely home to East Cowes with only a hand bearing compass which he carried at sea at all times. They arrived into Cowes on the Sabbath. The sailing yacht, with much seawater below, all the provisions was waterlogged.

However, back to Sunday morning October 1931: The only boat left on board Xarifa was the yacht's 13ft dinghy. My uncle Albert, and sailorman Phil Williams, of Endeavour II fame, on landing at Cowes to try and purchase some provisions, were almost arrested for being drunk: This was not the case. Their sea legs were not yet accustomed to dry land. The shops were all closed, being Sunday, but the police at Cowes were most kind and helpful when realising the true situation; being their safe arrival back to England. The police requested that some of the good shopkeepers of Cowes open their doors and cater for the needs of the crew. A point of nautical interest; the daughter of Samuel White, with whom I often enjoyed nautical yarns together with her pleasant husband.

Mr. Harry Spencer of Cowes, Isle of Wight, gentlemen photographer Mr. Keith Beken and his son Kenneth, manager Mr Mumford, and all members of staff of the Beken photographic business, still in existence at the time of going to press, are always a joy to see, together with the Beken collection. I consider it an honour that Mr. Keith Beken has written the foreword for my main maritime history book, which must be essential reading in all maritime homes, nation wide: This names every mariner and does not just call them East, West or South Coast crew members.

Percy Cook's daughter lost all her father's photographs during the 1953 floods. On my recent sending to the lady a photograph of the Xarifa crew, her kind words were as follows: 'Many, many

Schooner Xarifa Crew 1931
Captain Dickerson - Warsash, First Mate Bert Gladdin - Cowes, Isle of Wight, Chief Engineer Mr Groves - Cowes, Isle of Wight. Second engineer Mr. Denning - Cowes, Isle of Wight. Dan Mann, Aldeburgh, sadly drowned in February 1953 floods when the sea wall collapsed, Bill Mahoney - Gosport. Olly Chambers - Cowes. Edward Young - Cowes. Billy Bray - Padstowe. Ralph Couch - Port Isaac. Tom Fuger - Warsash. Ted Pannel - Warsash. Jimmy Hazel - Emsworth. Avery Woods - Warsash, Tom Edwards - Lower Swanick, (front row) Brothers Sam & Bill Diaper - River Itchen who served Meteors and Shamrocks - they were A1 sailormen, Chief Steward - Mr Bannister, Cowes, Second Steward - A Jefferies, Brightlingseas, Chef - Percy Cook, Aldeburgh.

They are all gone now, but not forgotten. And I am certain all my kind readers, together with family members of our mariners, will agree: 'their memory liveth on'.

thanks, for me this unique piece of my family history is beyond price' (V. Cook).

Frank Cross, A1 sailorman of East Cowes, aged 58 years in 1940, was strolling through East Cowes Park upon his eldest daughter's wedding day, a Saturday morning, when most tragically and sadly he was killed by a little boy's toy arrow, which struck him in the eye. I still visit all his family members. God bless all their memory.

It saddens me to say, in 1996, a features editor from The Southampton Echo, once said to my friend Ken Wheeler and I 'what do you think you know of yachting?' Needless to say Ken's grandfather's grave is HMS Marlborough, a 1924 wooden-walled shipping tragedy. Also, his father perished whilst rowing out to the Schooner Westward, November 1944, whilst saving two fellow seafarers: It was blowing hells, bells and saucepan lids.

My friend, skipper Malcolm Macgregor, was for many years a smack owner, a retired fisherman, oysterman, plus Priors Coasting Master. Back to approx. 1972, Malcolm and his brother Ian, along with Mr. Tom Gray, and sailing bargeman, Mr. Sid Westward, worked a fishing boat dredging for oysters between Calshot spit and Beaughleigh River: They were working for Mr. Christopher Kerrison who owns the leasehold rights in our local river Colne. I myself still remain a Freeman of Royal Charter Birthright. (not that it counts for much these days).

Malcolm and Ian were, indeed, very good friends of the lovely grand old characters sailormen brothers William and Tom Fuger, of Weather Birth, Warsash. They owned a lovely River Itchen gaffer rigged fishing smack. This was built many years past for the Reverend of the river Hamble. William and Tom had served the Shamrocks and still fished for government and Admiralty personnel when fish were plentiful during the second world war. Mr. Bobby Stoker of West Mersea, also in 1971, took his fishing craft down the glorious Hamble river, oyster catching.

JOHN S. BLYTHE
LT/COL. USAF RETIRED

After reading the first edition of my historical maritime book, John Blyth, who was featured in the book (see page 44), kindly wrote:

Dear John,

I thoroughly enjoyed your book and all the maritime history. You have done a wonderful job of collecting and writing such interesting stories filled with facts and events of by-gone years. You made interesting a subject that many of us know little or nothing about. The men of Brightlingsea were very much involved even though much of it took place in the Southampton area.

Also, the information about the Barquentine Galena (foundered November 13 1903). As a boy, I remember the Peter Iredale. We have been going to the Oregon coast since the late 1920's. In fact, Virginia and I were at Seaside about two months ago.

A film crew came to the house about three months ago and made a documentary on me. The director had found the tail number on the internet of a Spitfire that I had belly-landed in 1944 and asked if I would be interviewed. I agreed since most people don't know that the RAF and USAAC flew lone, unarmed aircraft to take photos of enemy targets. It has been shown in Melbourne and Edinborough and now has been accepted at the top American film festival. If you have a DVD I will send you a copy when it is released for public showing.

John, your work is invaluable for present and future generations.

Sincerely,

John S. Blyth

December 2006

R.R.C Britannia 1932. Most treasured and sacred memories. Back Row (L-R) Sailor H. Goldsmith of Olbra. W. Baily of Clacton, sailor 4th, Jack Holland of Brightlingsea served ten seasons Foc's'le cook, 1926-1936. Front Row (L-R), Tom Harvey of Wivenhoe, Launchman and Sailor. Centre, Johnny Turner of Wivenhoe, Mastheadsman. The task was 170 feet above the deck, a position Johnny, my friend well loved. Sailorman Archie Friend, of Brixham; his brother, Sailorman and 2nd mate, Ernie Friend, who on Easter Monday 1932 during racing, and with a strong wind was, sadly washed overboard and drowned from the lee scupper off Seaview I.O.W. His body was discovered nine days later by Captain Jim Gilby and crew. Also, brilliant sailormen from Emsworth, serving on board the J. Class Candida.

R.R.C.Britannia, jovial serving crew, Smoke O. Note the fine sail hoisted to dry, laying at Cowes I.O.W. home of the famous yachting regatta.

R.R.C. Britannia photograph 1932. 2nd mate Sam Shears of Brixham, sailorman who took over the position after the heroic sailorman Ernie Friend, also of Brixham, who was tragically washed overboard, and drowned, from the lee side scupper, Easter Monday 1933, whilst racing.

R.R.C. Britannia regular serving crew members Foc'le cooks. On the left, Bill Blackwood of Wivenhoe, and on the right Jack Holland of Brightlingsea, both sailormen with ten years loyal service, 1926-1936. During the winter months they would serve onboard White Star shipping company ships and were nice men to know for a nautical yarn.

Left: R.R.C. Britannia regular serving crew members in launch, Tom Harvey and Fred Turner of Wivenhoe, Tom serving as launchman sailor and Fred serving as sternsheetsman sailor, both jovial characters.

Above: R.R.C. Britannia, Wivenhoe sailors Tom Harvey and Fred Turner working on the boom end, a most heroic task.

Left: R.R.C. Britannia, fitting out at Marvin's Yard, Cowes I.O.W. 1935.

Below: Master of R.R.C. Britannia Captain Albert Turner M.V.O. of Wivenhoe, with his lady wife, Annie, in 1930.

Top Left: Two famous yachts, RRC Britannia (background) and RS Westwood (foreground), at Lymington Regatta 28 July 1933 during the first race of the season for big yachts.

Top Right: Shamrock photographed from the deck of RS Westwood competing in the Royal Southampton Yacht Club's Regatta, Cowes, Isle of White, 1934, in the race for the big boats, which was won by the King's Britannia.

Left: William Aldus,1st Mate, RS Westwood

Below: Westwood crew, Capt. Alf Diaper and 1st Mate William Aldus, twenty six years loyal service to owner and yacht. Whilst racing, Westwood carried ten apprentices for seamanship.

Left: Shamrock IV 1914. RUYC. Sir Thomas Lipton was the greatest sportsman and loser upon god's earth. He was a lifelong member of the royal Ulster Yacht Club. And it was not until his eightieth year, whilst lying in his death bed, that he was made a member of the Royal Yacht Squadron: This, despite him creating a wealth of employment in yacht building and sailing in his endeavours to regain the America's Cup to our shores.

The Queen Elizabeth II on board HMS Vanguard, circa 1950.

Photo by Sailmaker, the late Steven Ratsey of Cowes IOW, and given to JJ by his lady wife, Rachel, during a happy hour at the London Boat Show in 1987.

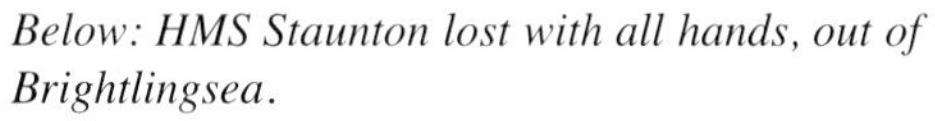

Below: HMS Staunton lost with all hands, out of Brightlingsea.

Captain Ben Parker along with his 1905 gallant serving crew members R.I. on board H.I.M. Kaiser William Emperor of Germany Racing Yacht Meteor. This photograph was taken in Hamburg. Allowed to J.J. from hanging upon a rusty nail within a River Itchen, old mariners home, circa 1950.

Meteor H.I.M. The German Emperor.

TOLLESBURY SMACKS OF YEARS AGO

NAME	REG. NO	OWNER	NAME	REG. NO	OWNER
GEM	C.K. 110	John Gurton	SECRET	C K. 109	J. Leavett
BETSY	C.K. 81	Alfred Frost	KINGFISHER	C.K. 7	Billy Redgwell
EMILY	C.K. 69	Steve Appleton	SUNBEAM	C.K. 328	J. Redhouse
WILLIAM & MARY	C.K. 90	Farrow	BLANCHE	C.K. 302	C. Rice
AMY	C.K. 15	Mark Kent	VALKYRIE	C.K. 426	H. Wilkinson
MARGARET	C.K. 192	Joseph Heard	PETREL	C.K. 2	R. Wilkinson
VOLANT (I)	C.K.	Louis Heard	MATCHLESS	C.K. 308	I. Rice
MARGARET	C.K. 204	William Crabb	LILY	C.K. 327	T. Frost
LARK	C.K. 114	John Heard	THISTLE	C.K. 324	Chas. Leavett
GLEANER	C.K. 108	John Heard	BOY KENNETH	C.K. 9	G. Brand
RUBINA	C.K. 83	W. Leavett	EXPRESS II	C.K. 231	A. Potter
KITTEN	C.K.	Fredk. Banyard	FLETT	C.K. 72	G. D. Lewis
EMMA	C.K. 369	W. Heard	ETHEL	C.K. 315	A. Lewis
VIOLET	C.K. 297	Geol Green	EILEEN	C.K.	W. Heard
ALMA	C.K.	Henry Stokes	MIRANDA	C.K. 282	C. Lewis
ACTIVE	C.K. 106	E. Dines	EDWARD & EMILY	C.K. 295	Zach Lewis
LAURA	S.M. 476	R. Page	RIPPLE	C.K.	L. Lewis
ALICE	C.K. 105	C. Wombwell	DEFIANCE	C.K. 97	John Lewis
FAME	C.K.	Mrs Bowles	EMILY	C.K. 91	R. Holder
ETHEL MAY	C.K. 262	Wm. Binks	WONDER	C.K. 116	W. Hodler
FLORENCE	C.K. 338	Robert Rose	BIANCA	C.K.	F. Holder
EXPRESS	C.K. 231	H. Appleton	MYSTERY	C.K.	J. Clark
EDITH	C.K. 251	H. Appleton	JAMES & MARY	C.K. 112	J. Barbrook
ALARM	C.K. 205	H. Appleton	BOADICEA	C.K. 113	J. Binks
LAURA Vera (or Varl)	C.K.	H. Appleton	JOHN HANNAH	C.K. 99	W. Potter
FAITH	C.K. 82	Richard Lewis	CHARLOTTE	C.K.	Ben Heard
PRIDE	C.K. 100	Sam Lewis	DOVE	C.K. 111	J. Pearce
WAVE	C K.	Alfred Lewis	EMMA JANE	C.K.	J. Bowles
M.K:T.	C.K. 280	John Townsend	BETHEL	C.K.	
HARRIET	C.K. 92	H. Beadle	DAISY	C.K. 6	Redhouse
RIPPLE	C.K. 201	R. Frost	JUNE	C.K. 98	John Lewis
VILLAGE BELLE	C.K. 138	R. Frost	GEORGE JAMES	C.K. 206	V. Fisher
ELIZABETH	C.K. 227	R. Frost	FROLIC	C.K. 18	G. Gurton
SECRET	C.K.	P. Frost	WATERLILY	C.K. 298	J. Hume
PROTECTION	C.K. 104	A. Leavett	EDITH FRANCES	C.K. 73	G. Heard
IREX	C.K. 152	A. Carter	HARRIET BLANCHE	C.K. 9	G. Heard
PROVIDENCE	C.K. 113	A. Carter	JENNY	C.K. 292	W. Burrows
PHANTOM	C.K. 175	John Gurton	SARAH	C.K.	H. Myall
MARIA ANN	C.K.	H. Frost	KATE ANN	C.K.	W. Hawes
EMMA AMELIA	C.K. 150	I. Leavett	LAURA	C.K. 42	W. Hawes
MY KATE	C.K. 25	W. Howe	JOHN EMMA	C.K. 96	G. Clark
HAROLD	C.K. 94	J. Bowles	JAMES & EMMA	C.K. 134	C. Pewter
ADVANCE	C.K.	J. Bowles	MARY	C.K. 78	A. Chatterson
MOLLY	C.K. 22	G. Heard	PEARL	C.K. 133	A. Chatterson
ALBERTA	C.K. 318	W. Pettican	ROSETTE	C.K. 93	G. Fisher
TRIUMPH	C.K.	W. Pettican	ALMA	C.K. 207	T. Lewis
CREEKSEA		J. Mills	POMONA	C.K. 9	T. Lewis
GLADYS	C.K. 77	J. Mills	ETHEL ALICE	C.K. 476	T. Lewis
CORSAIR	C.K. 444	Wrn. Collins	JULIA	C.K. 23	C. Frost
FLY		J. Drake	LUCY	C.K. 110	U. Lewis
WILLIAM ELIZA		W. Drake	ADC	C.K. 53	A. Barbrook
WILLIAM & EMILY	C.K. 212	Drake Brothers	ROSENA	C.K. 65	E. Heard
MARIA	C.K. 21	V. Leavett	PARAGON	C.K.	S. Barbrook
TIARA	C.K. 208	J. Wombwell	CHARLOTTE	C.K. 257	J. Ingate
EILEEN	C.K. 222	J. Heard	VOLANTE (II)	C.K. 88	Ben Heard
FANCY	C.K. 44	A. Lufkin	MAGNOLIA	C.K.	R. Appleton

Acknowledgements

First and Foremost, My Wife Jean, for her tolerance towards my lifetimes works and Maritime recordings

Mr Keith Beken & Son Kenneth, Company Director
Company Director, Mr Mumford
Mrs Anne Maria Hartrage and all members of staff of Beken, Cowes I.O.W.
Mr Harry Spencer of Spencer Rigging and Design Cowes I.O.W. and Southampton
Friend Mr Peter Martin, Martin Rigging, Lower Swanwick, Southampton
Mr Danny Houston, Editor and Team of CLASSIC BOAT
Mrs Ethel Harfield, Auntie Nee Diaper, River Itchen
Late Mr Steven Ratsey and Mrs Rachael Ratsey Sailmakers Cowes I.O.W.
Late Endeavour Sailorman and Lady Wife Mr and Mrs Phil and Vera Williams
Son Colin and Wife June, Southampton
Cllr Terry Sutton, The Worshipful The Mayor of Colchester 2005
Cllr Ron Levy, Colchester Borough Councillor
Mrs Rene Lucas, ex-owner of the restored Lulworth
Bruce Moss RHYC, Hon Historian and Archivist

Late Endeavour friend Ted Heard Junior of Tolleshury
And all sailormen, plus family members within for help and support to these works and recordings
Mr Terry Pengelley Looe, Mrs Tessa Daines Curator, until 2006 Emsworth Maritime Museum & Historical Trust
Lord Amherst, The Commodore of The Royal Yacht Squadron, Cowes I.O.W.
Maldwin Drummond OBE, DL, Hon, DSc. FSA also Historian and Past Commodore of RYS

Late Mr Johnny Fieldgate local, Mr Robin Cranfield of Rowhedge, Mr John Sharp
Mr John Pitt
Mr Alan Bines
Mr Desmond Summers
Mr Roger Hodgkinson
Mr Tommy Wright; Mariner Chief Engineer Retired Friend and shipmate
Mr Claude Dove
Mrs Jacqueline Maynard
Mr Steve Sleigh - Mail Boxes Etc. and members of Staff, Colchester
Mr John Dalziel, Photographer friend
Mr Steven Ratsey (sailmaker) and his lady wife, Rachel

May God Bless One and All
To whom have made this book possible.

Sincerely J. A. Jefferies

Front Cover Photograph:
King George V at the helm of RRC Britannia